IT Career Guide for Beginners

Steps to Launch and Develop a Successful Career in Information Technology

Chandraish Sinha

Legal Notes

Copyright © 2025 Books District Publication
First Edition
ISBN: 978-0-9992449-7-5

All rights reserved. No part of this book may be reproduced, stored in a retrieval system, copied, printed, modified, or shared by any means without prior written permission from the author, except for brief quotations used in critical articles or reviews.

Every effort has been made to ensure this book is complete and accurate. However, errors—both typographical and factual—may remain. The information is provided "as is" without any express or implied warranty. The author and publisher disclaim liability for any damages—actual or alleged—that may result from the use of this material.

This book is intended as a general guide and not a definitive source for IT career decisions. Some topics may resemble those in other works due to the shared nature of the subject matter.

Dedication

To my wife and daughter — for your love, patience, and belief in me. To every learner who took the first step — even when it felt uncertain.

To the educators, mentors, and trainers who light the path for others. This book is for those who keep going.

About the Author

Chandraish Sinha is the Founder and President of Ohio Computer Academy, an organization dedicated to practical, real-world IT education.

A lifelong advocate for technology training, Chandraish lives by his company's motto: Inspire, Educate, and Evolve. He specializes in Business Intelligence and has over 22 years of experience delivering scalable analytics and dashboarding solutions.

His work spans a wide range of BI tools, including Tableau, Power BI, QlikView, Qlik Sense, IBM Cognos, Business Objects, and Actuate. With a passion for data and problem-solving, he continues to explore platforms that drive deeper insight and decision-making.

Chandraish is also a published author with several books on dashboarding and data tools. His Amazon author page can be found at https://amazon.com/author/chandraishsinha.

He actively shares tips and tutorials through his blogs:
- Ohio Computer Academy Blog (https://ohiocomputeracademy.com/blogs/)
- Learn Tableau Public (https://www.learntableaupublic.com/)
- Learn All BI (https://www.learnallbi.com/)

Connect with him on LinkedIn: linkedin.com/in/chandraishsinha

Other Books by the Author

1. Tableau for Job Seekers
2. Excel Basics to Advanced
3. Dashboarding with Tableau
4. Mastering Power BI (Second Edition)
5. Mastering Power BI (First Edition)
6. Tableau Unlimited
7. Implementing Tableau Server
8. QlikView Essentials
9. QlikView Questions and Answers: Guide to QlikView and FAQs
10. Tableau 10 for Beginners
11. Tableau Dashboards: Step-by-Step Guide to Developing Visualizations in Tableau 9.2
12. Tableau Questions and Answers: Guide to Tableau Concepts and FAQs
13. How to Be a Successful IT Professional in the USA: A Checklist and Easy Guide to Success

Acknowledgments

My heartfelt thanks to all the readers who have supported my books over the years. Your reviews, messages, and feedback continue to inspire me to write and teach with greater clarity and purpose.

I'm grateful to the global IT community — educators, bloggers, YouTubers, and professionals — whose generous sharing of knowledge has made learning more accessible than ever.

A special thanks to the students and learners at Ohio Computer Academy, whose curiosity, commitment, and questions helped shape the practical focus of this book. Every workshop and discussion added real-world relevance to the content you now hold.

To the dedicated team at Ohio Computer Academy, thank you for your support, collaboration, and belief in our mission to inspire, educate, and evolve.

And most importantly, to my wife and daughter — thank you for your patience, encouragement, and love throughout this journey.

Preface

Information Technology is one of the most dynamic and rewarding fields today — but for beginners, figuring out where to start can feel overwhelming. It's easy to feel lost with so many roles, tools, certifications, and conflicting advice online. This book was written to provide clarity.

It's for students exploring their first step into tech, professionals switching careers, and anyone ready to build a real, long-term path in IT — whether in technical roles like cloud, data, and cybersecurity, or in non-coding roles like product support, business analysis, or project coordination.

Through my work with hundreds of learners and organizations, I've heard the same questions over and over:

- Where do I start?
- What does each IT career path involve?
- What skills should I learn — and in what order?
- How can I gain real-world experience if I don't have a job title yet?

This book was created to answer those questions — clearly, practically, and without the hype. Whether you're coming from a non-tech background, are self-taught, or have some experience but feel stuck, this guide meets you where you are. It explains how the IT industry works, outlines real career paths, highlights key tools and skills, and shows how to move from learning to practical application — all in a step-by-step format without guesswork. You'll also find checklists, career maps, learning plans, and free resources to help you stay focused and take action.

Technology evolves quickly. But careers are built slowly with consistent, focused learning. I hope this guide brings clarity, intention, and confidence to your journey into tech.

Over the 10 chapters in this book, you will learn the following:

Chapter 1: Getting Started in IT

This chapter will make you understand what IT work actually involves, assess if it aligns with your strengths and interests, and learn how to take your very first step into the field.

Chapter 2: The IT Landscape

Through this chapter, you get a clear overview of what Information Technology is, the key functions within IT, and the major job categories that power the industry.

Chapter 3: IT Employers and Industry Trends

In this chapter, you will learn about the types of companies that hire IT talent, how different industries apply technology, and which trends are shaping the future of tech careers.

Chapter 4: Career Paths in IT

This chapter explores various IT career paths in depth — from support to cybersecurity to data analytics — and what each path involves, including skills and tools.

Chapter 5: Building Skills for IT Career Paths

Through this chapter, you will understand exactly what to learn (and in what order) based on your chosen career path. It includes learning roadmaps for the key IT domains.

Chapter 6: Learning Methods and Certifications

This chapter explores key learning methods, how to choose the right type of training, and which certifications hold real value in today's job market.

Chapter 7: Turn Learning into Action

From this chapter, you will learn how to build a focused 12-week learning plan, gain experience even before your first job, and avoid common learning pitfalls.

Chapter 8: Preparing for the Job Market

This chapter teaches you to build a job-ready resume, set up your LinkedIn profile, prepare for interviews, and how to approach job applications strategically.

Chapter 9: Advancing a Career in IT

In this chapter, you will learn how to grow in your role, set long-term career goals, stay relevant, and pursue specialization as you build a sustainable tech career.

Chapter 10: AI Literacy for Tech Careers

This chapter will give you a practical understanding of how artificial intelligence is reshaping the IT landscape — and how to work with it, not compete against it. You will learn to use tools like ChatGPT, Gemini, and GitHub Copilot to support your learning, productivity, and career growth.

In addition to the 10 chapters, the book also includes a Glossary of Common IT Terms for quick reference and an Appendix with curated free learning tools by career path, to help you take action right away.

Errata

While every effort has been made to ensure accuracy and clarity in this book, occasional errors may have slipped through. If you find anything unclear or incorrect, please email:
hello@BooksDistrict.com
Subject line: Errata – IT Career Guide for Beginners
Your feedback is appreciated and helps improve future editions.

Table of Contents

1. **Getting Started In IT** 1
   Introduction 1
   The Nature of IT Work 2
      Common Elements in IT Work 2
      It's Not All Coding 3
      What IT Means for Beginners 3
   Is IT Right for You? 4
   Essential Skills to Get Started 5
   Taking the First Step 7
   Conclusion 8
   Frequently Asked Questions 8
   Quick Checklist 10

2. **The IT Landscape** 11
   Introduction 11
   What is Information Technology (IT)? 11
      The Real Role of IT 12
      Who are IT Professionals? 12
   Key IT Functions by Complexity 13
   Major IT Job Categories 17
      Support and Operations 17
      Quality Assurance and Testing 18
      Non-coding Tech Roles 19
      Software and Web Development 21
      Data Management and Analytics 22
      AI and Machine Learning 23
      Infrastructure and System Management 24
      Cloud Computing 25
      Automation and DevOps 26
      Cybersecurity 27

　　　　System Architecture *28*
　　　Conclusion 30
　　　Frequently Asked Questions 30
　　　Quick Checklist 32

3. **IT Employers And Industry Trends** 33
　　　Introduction 33
　　　Types of IT Employers 33
　　　　Tech Companies *34*
　　　　Large Enterprises *34*
　　　　Startups *34*
　　　　Consulting Firms and System Integrators *35*
　　　　Governments and Nonprofit Organizations *35*
　　　IT across Industries 35
　　　　Finance and Banking *36*
　　　　Healthcare *36*
　　　　Retail and E-commerce *36*
　　　　Artificial Intelligence in Industry *37*
　　　　Education and EdTech *37*
　　　　Manufacturing and Supply Chain *38*
　　　　Government and Public Sector *38*
　　　Emerging IT Trends 38
　　　　Cloud and Remote Infrastructure *39*
　　　　Cybersecurity as a Core Priority *39*
　　　　The Rise of Software and Web Development *39*
　　　　AI, Automation, and Intelligent Systems *40*
　　　　Data Analytics, Visualization, and Reporting .. *40*
　　　　Cross-functional Technologists with Business Awareness *41*
　　　Conclusion 41
　　　Frequently Asked Questions 42
　　　Quick Checklist 43

4. **Career Paths In IT** 45
   Introduction 45
   Career Path: Support and Operations 46
   Career Path: Quality Assurance and Testing 47
   Career Path: Non-coding Tech Roles 48
   Career Path: Software and Web Development 50
   Career Path: Data Management and Analytics 52
   Career Path: AI and Machine Learning 53
   Career Path: Infrastructure and System Management 55
   Career Path: Cloud Computing 56
   Career Path: Automation and DevOps 58
   Career Path: Cybersecurity 59
   Career Path: System Architecture 60
   Conclusion 62
   Frequently Asked Questions 63
   Quick Checklist 64

5. **Building Skills For IT Career Paths** 65
   Introduction 65
   Skill Path: Support and Operations 66
   Skill Path: Quality Assurance and Testing 67
   Skill Path: Non-coding Tech Roles 69
   Skill Path: Software and Web Development 71
   Skill Path: Data Management and Analytics 74
   Skill Path: AI and Machine Learning 76
   Skill Path: Infrastructure and System Management 77
   Skill Path: Cloud Computing 79
   Skill Path: Automation and DevOps 82
   Skill Path: Cybersecurity 84
   Skill Path: System Architecture 86
   Conclusion 88
   Frequently Asked Questions 88

Quick Checklist 89

6. Learning Methods And Certifications 91

Introduction 91
Learning Options: What Works and Why 91
    Self-paced Learning (Online Courses, YouTube, and Blogs) 92
    Instructor-led or Structured Training 92
    Bootcamps (Online or In-Person) 92
    Community Colleges or University Programs 93
    Choosing a Learning Format 94
Certifications That Matter 94
    Role-relevant Certifications 96
Conclusion 106
Frequently Asked Questions 106
Quick Checklist 108

7. Turn Learning Into Action 109

Introduction 109
Building a Learning Plan 109
Pitfalls to Avoid While Learning 113
How to Gain Experience Without a Job 115
What If You Fall Off Track? 116
Conclusion 117
Frequently Asked Questions 118
Quick Checklist 119

8. Preparing For The Job Market 121

Introduction 121
Building a Job-Ready Resume 121
    What makes a Strong resume? 122
    Crafting a Resume 123
    Sample Resume 123
Using LinkedIn to Get Noticed 125
    Sample Beginner LinkedIn "About" Section 127

Preparing for Interviews 127
    What to Expect in IT Interviews *128*
    Mastering the Interview Process *129*
    Interview Formats and Preparation Tips *130*
    End-of-Interview Questions *131*
Finding IT Job Opportunities 131
Navigating the Job Hunt 133
    Reading a Job Description *133*
    Applying for a Job Strategically *134*
    Dealing with Rejections *134*
Conclusion 135
Frequently Asked Questions 135
Quick Checklist 137

9. Advancing A Career In IT 139
Introduction 139
Staying Relevant 139
Advancing in the Current Role 141
Pursuing Specialization 142
Setting and Tracking Career Goals 143
Conclusion 145
Frequently Asked Questions 145
Quick Checklist 146

10. AI Literacy For Tech Careers 149
Introduction 149
Introducing AI Literacy 150
    Practical Uses of AI *150*
    Top AI Tools for Learning and Productivity *151*
    Getting started with the AI Tool *152*
Prompting Basics 153
    Basic Prompt formula *153*
    Examples by use case *154*

Common Pitfalls to Avoid...........154
AI as a Learning Companion............154
Conclusion 156
Frequently Asked Questions 156
Quick Checklist 157
Final Thoughts 157

GLOSSARY OF COMMON IT TERMS............159

APPENDIX: FREE LEARNING TOOLS AND RESOURCES BY CAREER PATH............163

INDEX 167-175

How to Use This Book

Information Technology (IT) is a vast and fast-moving field, full of opportunities, and just as full of confusion.

There are countless career paths and specializations: networking, cybersecurity, cloud, data, development, AI, and more. For someone new to the field, this can feel overwhelming.

As someone who interacts regularly with students, career changers, and aspiring IT professionals, I've noticed a common challenge: most people don't know where to start or what direction to follow. There's no shortage of advice out there, but that's part of the problem. Blogs, YouTube channels, social media, and forums all offer different, often conflicting opinions.

Some promote cloud computing. Others recommend data science or AI. One side argues for college degrees; the other champions' bootcamps or self-study. The result? Uncertainty, wasted time, and people giving up before they even begin.

This constant noise makes it harder, not easier, for beginners to make informed decisions. It creates pressure, doubt, and wasted time chasing the "hot trend" instead of building a solid foundation.

Here's what most people won't tell you:
There is no single, guaranteed path to success in IT. But there is a smarter, more strategic way to move forward — one that aligns with your strengths, your interests, and the way the industry actually works.

That's what this book is about.

What This Book Is (and Isn't)

This book isn't about becoming a coding genius in 30 days or landing a job at a big-name tech company with zero experience. Instead, it gives you a real-world roadmap to help you:
- Choose a career track that aligns with your goals
- Learn and build the right skills
- Gain real experience, even without a job title
- Prepare for the job market
- Grow your career for the long term

Each chapter focuses on a key stage of this journey, with clear steps, real examples, and practical insights.

Who This Book Is For

This book is for anyone who wants to build a real, lasting career in IT — not just land a job, but actually grow in the field, stay relevant, and feel confident navigating it long-term.
- A student or recent graduate trying to get their foot in the door
- A career switcher from a non-tech background, looking for clarity and direction
- A self-taught learner wondering if you're on the right track
- An early-stage IT professional who feels stuck or unsure about the next step

Whether you're technical or non-technical, just starting out or trying to level up, this book is built to guide you — step by step — through the decisions, skills, and strategies that lead to long-term success in tech.

How to Navigate This Book

The book is designed to be read in order, but you don't have to. If you already know your track, jump to the skill paths. If you're job hunting, go straight to resume building or interview preparation. No matter where you start, the book provides:

- Step-by-step guidance
- Real-world examples
- Actionable checklists
- Optional downloadable resources
- Each chapter ends with an FAQ and quick checklist to help reinforce your understanding and actions
- Tool comparisons are included to help you choose between common options like AWS vs Azure, Tableau vs Power BI, and others
- A Glossary at the end of the book explains key IT terms in plain language
- The Appendix includes a curated list of free learning tools, trial software, and resources by career path
- Use the included Learning Planner and Project Log to track weekly goals and showcase real-world projects

Don't aim for perfection. Aim for progress. Start where you are. Learn what's next. Keep moving. That's how real careers are built — one smart, consistent step at a time.

CHAPTER 1

Getting Started in IT

Introduction

Breaking into the world of Information Technology can feel both exciting and overwhelming. There are numerous career paths, hundreds of tools, and a steady stream of advice online urging you to "learn to code" or "get certified fast." But where do you actually begin?

This chapter is designed for true beginners — people who are considering a career in IT but aren't sure what it involves, whether they're a good fit, or how to take the first step. You don't need a computer science degree or years of experience. What you need is a starting point.

In this chapter, we'll walk through how to explore your interest in IT, build basic digital skills, and get a feel for what it's like to work in the tech industry. You'll also learn what tools to try, how to test your aptitude, and how to decide whether this is the right direction for you — before committing to a specific track.

This chapter will cover the following topics:
- The Nature of IT Work
- Is IT right for you?
- Essential skills to get started
- Taking the first step

The Nature of IT Work

IT work isn't just about sitting behind a computer writing code — and it's not always as technical or intimidating as it might seem from the outside. While technology is at the center, most IT roles are built around solving problems, supporting users, improving systems, and helping organizations work more efficiently.

At its core, working in IT means using tools, logic, and communication to keep things running or make them better.

Common Elements in IT Work

While each career path is different, there are some common threads across most of the IT roles, which are as follows:

- **Problem solving**: Whether it's fixing a system error, debugging a program, or improving a workflow, IT work involves identifying issues and figuring out how to resolve them.
- **Working with tools**: Most IT professionals use a combination of tools — from Excel and ticketing systems to databases, cloud dashboards, or development environments.
- **Learning on the job**: Technology changes quickly. Staying up to date often means learning something new while working, not just beforehand.
- **Collaboration**: IT isn't done in isolation. Even technical roles require communicating with users, teammates, or stakeholders to gather information and deliver solutions.
- **Documentation and process**: Writing things down, following checklists, updating logs — these are all part of making sure that the systems stay stable and others can follow your work.

It's Not All Coding

A common misconception is that everyone in IT needs to know Coding. That's not true. Many roles focus on configuration, analysis, support, testing, and management. While programming can open doors, it's not the only way to contribute to the tech world.

What IT Means for Beginners

If you're just starting out, expect to:
- Work with both people and systems
- Follow processes while learning how things connect
- Make mistakes (and learning from them)
- Build confidence through practice, not perfection

The goal isn't to master everything at once — it's to develop the habits and mindset that support continuous learning and meaningful contributions to your team, projects, and organization.

Now that you have a clearer picture of what IT work actually involves, it's worth taking a moment to reflect on whether this type of work aligns with your interests, mindset, and strengths. The next section will guide you in accomplishing that.

Is IT Right for You?

Before moving forward, let's take a moment to reflect on how your interests and mindset align with IT work.

The following list is designed to identify how well your interests, mindset, and habits align with a career in IT. There are no scores or right answers — just a simple way to get a clearer sense of fit before choosing a track.

S.No.	Statement	Yes	No	Not Sure
1.	Enjoy solving problems and figuring out how things work			
2.	Comfortable learning new software or digital tools			
3.	Able to follow step-by-step instructions			
4.	Curious about how apps and systems work			
5.	Enjoy organizing or analyzing information			
6.	Stay focused even when learning gets tough			
7.	Familiar with Word, Excel, or PowerPoint and open to improving those skills			
8.	Interested in a career with ongoing learning and growth			
9.	Prefer structured and logical thinking			
10.	Ready to dedicate time every week to learning new skills			

Table 1.1: Is IT Right for You?

If most responses fall under "Yes," that's a strong signal that an IT career could be a good fit for you. Success in technology isn't about being a genius — it's about curiosity, consistency, and a willingness to learn and grow over time.

Essential Skills to Get Started

Before choosing a career track or diving into certifications, it's important to build a basic foundation — the digital skills and thinking patterns that make it easier to learn and grow in any IT role.

You don't need advanced coding or technical experience to begin. But certain core skills will give you a head start and help you feel more confident as you explore. Some of them are discussed here:

- **Digital Literacy**
    - Navigating file systems (folders, extensions, shortcuts)
    - Using email professionally
    - Managing downloads, settings, and installations
    - Learning basic keyboard shortcuts
- **AI Literacy**
    - Exploring tools like ChatGPT, Gemini, or Copilot
    - Asking AI to explain technical topics in simple terms
    - Practicing how to write clear and useful prompts
    - Using AI to brainstorm ideas, check your writing, or summarize notes
    - Always reviewing AI output critically — it's helpful, not perfect
- **Microsoft Office Applications**
    - MS Word: formatting, document sharing, and using basic templates
    - PowerPoint: creating clear and simple presentations
    - Excel: Using formulas, pivot tables, charts, and data filters

> *Tip:* Excel is used everywhere —even in non-technical roles — for data analysis, automation, reporting, and testing. Learning formulas, filters, and pivot tables builds logical thinking and attention to detail. It's one skill that's valuable across all IT jobs.

- **Communication Skills**
    - Writing clearly and professionally
    - Explaining technical information in simple terms
    - Listening and asking the right questions
- **Problem-solving Mindset**
    - Breaking down problems into steps
    - Researching solutions (for example, searching error messages)
    - Testing and learning from mistakes
- **Basic Computer Troubleshooting**
    - Restarting systems and checking connectivity issues
    - Installing and uninstalling software
    - Understanding basic error messages
    - Managing system updates and antivirus tools
    - Using Task Manager (Windows) or Activity Monitor (Mac) to check performance
    - Connecting to Wi-Fi and diagnosing basic network issues
- **Introduction to Databases (Optional but Valuable)**
    - Understanding how data is stored, organized, and accessed
    - Build foundational logic useful for careers in data, testing, or IT support

> *Tip*: *Almost everything in IT is powered by databases, including websites, applications, reporting tools, and support systems. Learning SQL helps you understand how data is stored, searched, and connected behind the scenes. It's one of the most widely used skills across IT roles, and a strong foundation in it can open doors in analytics, QA, development, and many more.*

These skills don't need to be mastered all at once. Start with what's accessible — watch tutorials, take a beginner course, or simply practice using these tools daily. As comfort grows, you'll be better prepared to choose a track and move deeper into technical learning.

Taking the First Step

A career in IT doesn't begin with mastering everything at once — it begins with a small, focused action. Momentum builds by doing something simple, consistently.

The following are a few simple ways to begin:

- **Choose one skill**: Starting with Excel, basic troubleshooting, or computer fundamentals helps you establish a strong base.

- **Gain background knowledge**: Watching walkthroughs or tutorials online offers insight into how IT professionals approach tasks and tools.

- **Begin with a structured or self-paced course**: Platforms such as Coursera, Microsoft Learn, or YouTube offer free foundational content, while instructor-led training provides structure, accountability, and hands-on practice for those who prefer guided learning.

- **Seek out real-world context**: Talking with someone in tech or reading day-in-the-life articles helps make IT careers more tangible and less intimidating. Many institutes offer free consultations to help choose the right starting point — whether self-paced or instructor-led.

Whether it's exploring a tool, joining a course, or simply asking questions, each small action builds momentum. The key is to start — and keep going, one step at a time.

Conclusion

Getting started in IT isn't about being an expert on day one — it's about building a clear and realistic foundation. Understanding the nature of IT work, reflecting on personal fit, and focusing on essential skills are all powerful initial steps.

What's the most important takeaway? To get started, you don't need to know everything. Real progress will follow with curiosity, structure, and consistency.

In the next chapter, we'll explore how the IT world is structured — including the key functions, job categories, and how different career paths begin.

Frequently Asked Questions

1. Do I need a computer science degree to start a career in IT?

Ans. No. Many entry-level IT roles value skills and practical experience over formal degrees. Certifications, hands-on projects, and consistent learning matter more than credentials alone.

2. What's the best first skill to learn if I'm starting from zero?

Ans. Start with digital literacy and basic troubleshooting. Then build comfort with tools like Excel, PowerPoint, or simple scripting. These foundational skills apply across nearly all IT paths.

3. I'm not technical — can I still succeed in IT?

Ans. Yes. Many IT roles involve analysis, support, documentation, or coordination — not all require coding. If you're curious, logical, and willing to learn, you can find a track that fits you.

4. Should I learn coding right away?

Ans. Not necessarily. First, you need to learn the basics of how systems work. If you choose a development track later, you can dive into coding. Otherwise, roles in support, analysis, or cloud often don't require it.

5. How do I know if IT is really right for me?

Ans. Try small steps: follow tutorials, explore tools, or talk to people in tech. If you enjoy solving problems, learning independently, and using technology creatively, IT may be a good fit.

6. Is 12 weeks enough to become job-ready?

Ans. It's enough to build a foundation, but not to master everything. Think of 12 weeks as a launchpad — the beginning of a longer-term learning and career journey.

7. What if I feel overwhelmed by how fast things change in tech?

Ans. Everyone feels that way at first. Begin with one tool or topic and remain consistent. IT rewards curiosity and problem-solving, not knowing everything upfront.

Quick Checklist

Use this checklist to review your progress and track what you've done. Check off each item as you complete it.

☐ I understand what IT work actually involves (beyond just coding)

☐ I've reflected on whether IT aligns with my mindset and interests

☐ I've completed the "Is IT Right for You?" self-check

☐ I can describe basic IT work in terms of tools, problem-solving, and teamwork

☐ I've reviewed and understood core beginner skills such as:

☐ Digital literacy (folders, email, file management)

☐ Microsoft Office basics (especially Excel functions)

☐ Communication in a tech context

☐ A problem-solving approach

☐ Basic troubleshooting steps

☐ Optional: SQL/database introduction

☐ I've chosen one skill or tool to begin learning or practicing

☐ I've taken a first small action — downloaded a tool, signed up for a course, or tried a tutorial

☐ I feel more confident about exploring a career in IT

Tip: You don't need to check every box right now. Use this list as a progress tracker, and revisit it as you move forward.

CHAPTER 2

The IT Landscape

Introduction

This chapter offers a foundational view of the IT landscape — what it is, how it functions, and the range of roles and career paths it includes. Whether you're new to the field or exploring a transition, this chapter breaks down the essential components of working in IT today.

This chapter will cover the following topics:

- What is Information Technology (IT)?
- Key IT functions by complexity
- The major job categories in IT

What is Information Technology (IT)?

Information Technology (IT) is a broad discipline that forms the operational backbone of modern enterprises. It's more than just hardware or software — IT is a strategic enabler of business performance, innovation, and growth.

IT leverages computer systems and integrates areas such as systems architecture, application development, cloud computing, cybersecurity, and data operations. Together, these functions align technology with business objectives to drive efficiency, scalability, and resilience.

At its core, IT is about using technology to solve problems, manage data, and turn information into insights that support smarter decisions across every part of an organization.

The Real Role of IT

IT is fundamentally about managing and using information effectively, which includes:

- Collecting data from multiple sources
- Storing and securing that data
- Processing it to generate meaningful insights
- Sharing it across systems and teams in a secure and reliable way

Whether maintaining servers, writing code, analyzing data, or supporting end users — all of it contributes to that cycle. IT is not just about tech for its own sake — it's about making systems work better for people, teams, and organizations.

Broadly speaking, IT roles fall into two key areas:

- **Infrastructure and operations**: Supporting and maintaining the systems, networks, and platforms that keep things running.
- **Development and data**: Building, improving, and analyzing tools, systems, and software to help organizations grow and operate smarter.

Who are IT Professionals?

IT professionals plan, build, support, and secure the technology that keeps businesses operational. They come from diverse backgrounds and work in various roles — from system administrators and cloud engineers to data analysts, developers, and cybersecurity experts.

They share a problem-solving mindset, natural curiosity, and the ability to adapt to constant change. Some write code while others manage infrastructure. Many specialize in user support, project coordination, or translating business needs into technical solutions.

There is no one-size-fits-all profile for an IT professional, which makes the field accessible and diverse.

The wide range of roles in IT means there's no single profile for success — making it a field that welcomes many different strengths and backgrounds.

Key IT Functions by Complexity

Information Technology encompasses a wide range of functional areas, each contributing to the design, delivery, and maintenance of technology within organizations. The following section outlines these core functions, organized by their typical complexity level:

- **Support and Operations**
    - Helping end users with technical issues
    - Ensuring employees can work efficiently with the tools and systems in place
- **Quality Assurance and Testing**
    - Ensuring software, systems, and applications function as intended through structured testing processes
    - Identifying bugs, performance issues, and user experience problems before deployment
    - Creating manual and automated test cases
    - Supporting continuous testing in agile and DevOps environments for faster and more reliable releases
    - Maintaining product quality and reducing risk through early issue detection and resolution

- **Non-coding Tech Roles**
  - Bridging the gap between technical teams and business stakeholders to align goals, timelines, and expectations
  - Managing projects, products, and workflows
  - Gathering requirements, prioritizing features, and ensuring timely delivery of technology solutions
  - Translating complex technical concepts into clear business terms for decision makers
  - Supporting communication, planning, and coordination across teams in fast-moving IT environments
- **Software and Web Development**
  - Building software tools, web applications, and internal systems
  - Writing, testing, and maintaining code to automate tasks and deliver services
- **Data Management and Analytics**
  - Gathering, storing, and processing large volumes of data
  - Turning raw data into actionable insights
- **AI and Machine Learning**
  - Designing systems that learn from data to make predictions or decisions
  - Using tools like Python, TensorFlow, scikit-learn, or PyTorch
  - Building models for classification, forecasting, recommendation, or automation
  - Working closely with data engineers and analysts to prepare and feed structured datasets
  - Having a solid understanding of statistics, linear algebra, and programming

- **Infrastructure and System Management**
  - Managing physical hardware and networks
  - Setting up and maintaining operating systems and user environments
  - Ensuring uptime, speed, and availability of systems
- **Cloud Computing**
  - Managing infrastructure and applications on cloud platforms like AWS, Azure, or Google Cloud
  - Managing scalability, cost efficiency, and reliability in a virtual environment
- **Automation and DevOps**
  - Automating infrastructure provisioning, configuration, and deployment
  - Managing CI/CD (Continuous Integration and Continuous Deployment) pipelines to streamline software delivery
  - Ensuring code changes are automatically tested, integrated, and deployed to production environments
  - Bridging development and operations teams to improve collaboration, speed, and reliability
  - Supporting rapid, stable releases and rollback capabilities through automation and monitoring
- **Cybersecurity**
  - Protecting systems and data from threats, breaches, and attacks
  - Implementing security policies and monitoring activity
- **System Architecture**
  - Designing technical system structures and platforms that support business operations
  - Defining how different tools, databases, and services interact

The following table outlines IT functions by complexity level and typical entry path, offering a clear view of how professionals can grow through the field:

S.No.	IT Function	Complexity Level	Typical Entry Path
1.	Support and Operations	Beginner	Help Desk, Desktop Support
2.	Quality Assurance and Testing	Beginner to Intermediate	Manual QA, Junior Tester
3.	Non-coding Tech Roles	Beginner to Intermediate	Business Analyst, Coordinator, Junior PM
4.	Software and Web Development	Intermediate	Junior Developer, Web Developer
5.	Data Management and Analytics	Intermediate to Advanced	Data Analyst, SQL Developer, Excel
6.	AI and Machine Learning	Advanced	Junior Data Scientist, ML Intern, Research Assistant
7.	Infrastructure and System Management	Intermediate to Advanced	SysAdmin, Network Admin
8.	Cloud Computing	Advanced	Cloud Support Associate, Junior Cloud Engineer, Cloud Administrator
9.	Automation and DevOps	Advanced	Junior DevOps Engineer, CI/CD Intern, Release Coordinator
10.	Cybersecurity	Advanced	Security Analyst, SOC Analyst (Tier 1), Cybersecurity Intern
11.	System Architecture	Expert	Senior Engineer, Tech Lead

Table 2.1: IT Functions by Complexity and Entry Path

The core functions of IT form the foundation of how technology supports and drives modern organizations. From support and infrastructure to data, cloud, and security, every function plays a role in building systems that are efficient, scalable, and secure. Understanding these functions creates a solid base for exploring the job categories that bring them to life.

Major IT Job Categories

Now that the core functions are clear, this section explores the roles that deliver those functions in various organizations.

IT careers span a wide spectrum — from deeply technical engineering to strategic planning, communication, and end-user support. These categories help highlight how different skill sets align with specific roles and where strong growth opportunities exist across the industry.

Each category includes a brief overview, common job titles, and typical experience levels that help to clarify which paths align with different skills and career goals.

This overview sets the stage for choosing a direction that fits both current capabilities and long-term career ambitions.

Support and Operations

Support and Operations roles are often the first step into an IT career. These professionals are responsible for maintaining daily technical operations, helping users troubleshoot issues, and ensuring systems run smoothly. It's a hands-on category where foundational skills are built — from understanding user environments to working with hardware, software, and networks.

These roles offer valuable exposure to a broad range of tools and IT practices, making them an excellent starting point for specialization in areas such as networking, cybersecurity, or system administration.

Common roles in Support and Operations are:

- **Help Desk Technician/IT Support Specialist**: Provides first-line technical support to end users, solving issues related to hardware, software, network connectivity, and access.

- **Desktop Support Technician**: Works directly with users to install, configure, and troubleshoot desktops, laptops, printers, and related peripherals — either on-site or remotely.

- **IT Operations Specialist**: Oversees daily IT operations such as system checks, backups, patching, and basic network support. Often supports system administrators and escalates advanced issues.

- **NOC Technician (Network Operations Center)**: Monitors system performance and uptime. Responds to alerts and ensures quick resolution of infrastructure-related incidents.

- **IT Service Desk Analyst**: Coordinates ticket resolution, service requests, and incident management using platforms like ServiceNow or Jira.

Quality Assurance and Testing

Quality Assurance (QA) and Testing roles ensure that software and systems meet performance, reliability, and usability standards before being released. These professionals test applications to identify bugs, verify functionality, and ensure everything works as expected under different conditions.

QA roles exist throughout the development cycle and often collaborate with developers, product managers, and end users. There are opportunities in both manual and automated testing, making this a versatile area for both new and experienced professionals.

Common roles in Quality Assurance and Testing are:

- **Manual QA Tester / QA Analyst**: Executes test cases manually to verify that software functions as expected. Focuses on usability, functionality, and bug tracking. Ideal for identifying real-world issues during development.

- **Test Automation Engineer / QA Automation Engineer**: Builds and maintains automated test scripts using tools like Selenium to streamline regression and performance testing.

- **Performance Tester**: Tests software under different loads and conditions to measure speed, stability, and scalability. Uses tools like JMeter, LoadRunner, or custom scripts.

- **QA Lead / Test Manager**: Oversees the QA process, manages test teams, and ensures alignment with project timelines and quality goals.

Non-coding Tech Roles

Non-coding tech roles play a critical part in planning, coordinating, and delivering technology projects. These roles often act as the link between technical teams and business stakeholders, helping to ensure that solutions meet real needs and are delivered on time.

Professionals in this space focus on strategy, communication, coordination, analysis, and documentation. They are ideal for those who enjoy solving problems, organizing work, and working with cross-functional teams, without necessarily needing deep programming expertise.

Common non-coding tech roles are:

- **Technical Project Manager**: Oversees the planning and execution of IT projects. Manages schedules, resources, risk, and communication across cross-functional teams.

- **Program Manager**: Oversees multiple related projects, often aligning them with strategic goals. Focuses on cross-team coordination, budgets, and stakeholder management.

- **Product Manager**: Defines the vision, roadmap, and priorities for a product or feature. Gathers user feedback, writes product requirements, and works closely with development teams to bring ideas to life.

- **Technical Product Manager**: Similar to a Product Manager, but with deeper involvement in technical implementation. Acts as a bridge between engineering and business teams.

- **Business Analyst**: Gathers and analyzes business requirements, identifies problems or opportunities, and recommends IT solutions. Often involved in testing and validation as well.

- **Systems Analyst**: Focuses on evaluating and improving existing systems. Translates business needs into technical requirements and works with developers to implement changes.

- **Scrum Master**: Facilitates Agile development processes, removes blockers, and keeps teams aligned on sprint goals. Acts as a coach and process manager rather than a task owner.

- **Technical Writer**: Creates user guides, documentation, manuals, and knowledge base content to help users and teams understand and use technology effectively.

Software and Web Development

Software and web development roles are at the core of building the tools, platforms, and applications that power digital experiences. These professionals design, write, and maintain code that brings ideas to life — from internal systems to customer-facing products.

This category includes roles that focus on both the visual interface users interact with and the underlying systems that make those applications work. Developers work closely with designers, QA testers, product managers, and system architects to deliver scalable and maintainable solutions.

Common roles in Software and Web Development are:

- **Frontend Developer**: Builds the user interface (UI) of websites and applications — the part users interact with. Uses languages like HTML, CSS, and JavaScript frameworks (React, Angular, Vue).

- **Backend Developer**: Works on the server side — managing databases, APIs, and logic that power the application. Common languages include Python, Java, Node.js, Ruby, and PHP.

- **Full-stack Developer**: Handles both frontend and backend development.

- **Mobile Developer**: Builds applications for iOS and Android platforms. May specialize in native (Swift, Kotlin) or cross-platform tools like Flutter or React Native.

- **Software Engineer**: A broad role that applies engineering principles to software design and development. Often overlaps with backend or full-stack development in larger systems or enterprise apps.

- **UI/UX Designer**: Designs the look, feel, and flow of applications and websites. Works closely with frontend developers to ensure intuitive and user-friendly interfaces.

Data Management and Analytics

Data Management and Analytics roles are responsible for turning raw information into useful insights. These professionals design systems for storing and retrieving data, build pipelines for processing it, and create visualizations and models to support business decisions.

This category covers a wide range of roles — from those focused on data integrity and access to those working on predictive analytics and machine learning. It combines technical skills with analytical thinking, making it a strong career path for those who enjoy working with data to solve problems.

Common roles in Data Management and Analytics are:

- **Data Analyst**: Interprets data, builds reports, and identifies trends to support business decisions. Proficient in tools like Excel, SQL, Power BI, or Tableau.

- **Business Intelligence (BI) Analyst**: Focuses on creating dashboards and visualizations to monitor performance metrics. Works closely with stakeholders to translate data into strategy.

- **SQL Developer**: Specializes in writing complex SQL queries, stored procedures, and database scripts to support reporting, analytics, and application data layers. Works closely with data analysts, engineers, and application developers to ensure high-performance access to clean, structured data.

- **Data Engineer**: Builds and maintains data pipelines, warehouses, and ETL processes. Ensures data is clean, accessible, and ready for analysis.

- **Database Administrator (DBA)**: Manages and maintains databases, ensuring performance, backups, and data security. Often works with systems like MySQL, Oracle, or PostgreSQL.

- **Data Scientist**: Uses statistical methods, machine learning, and modeling to generate predictive insights. Often skilled in Python, R, and data science libraries.

- **Machine Learning Engineer**: Builds and deploys machine learning models into production environments. More focused on scalability, automation, and performance.

- **Data Steward / Data Quality Analyst**: Ensures data integrity, consistency, and compliance with data governance policies. Plays a key role in maintaining trustworthy data across systems.

AI and Machine Learning

AI and ML roles focus on building systems that can learn from data and make predictions or decisions without being explicitly programmed. These positions require strong analytical skills, a background in statistics or math, and the ability to work with large datasets and modern tools.

These roles often overlap with data science and engineering, and many professionals start in data-focused roles before transitioning into more specialized AI work.

Common roles under AI and Machine Learning are:

- **Machine Learning Engineer**: Designs, trains, and deploys ML models in production environments. Works with libraries like scikit-learn, TensorFlow, or PyTorch.

- **Data Scientist**: Explores datasets, builds statistical or predictive models, and communicates insights. Often, a hybrid role blends analytics and machine learning.

- **AI/ML Research Assistant**: Supports research teams by experimenting with algorithms, testing models, or contributing to academic and industry-focused projects.

- **NLP Engineer**: Focuses on natural language processing tasks such as text classification, sentiment analysis, or chatbots.

- **Computer Vision Engineer**: Develops systems that analyze images or video using AI, often in industries like healthcare, automotive, or manufacturing.

Infrastructure and System Management

Infrastructure and System Management roles focus on building, maintaining, and securing the core IT environment that supports an organization's operations. These professionals manage servers, networks, operating systems, and user access — the foundational layers on which applications and services run.

These roles require strong technical skills and a deep understanding of system performance, troubleshooting, and configuration. They often serve as a stepping stone to more specialized paths like cloud computing, cybersecurity, or systems architecture.

Common roles under Infrastructure and System Management are:

- **System Administrator**: Manages servers, operating systems, and user accounts; handles patches, updates, and troubleshooting. A Windows/Linux administrator also plays a part in this role and specializes in managing environments based on specific OS platforms.

- **Network Administrator**: Manages internal networks, routers, switches, and firewalls; ensures secure and stable connectivity.

- **IT Operations and Monitoring**: Monitors system and service health, handles escalations, and manages performance tools.

- **Infrastructure Engineer**: Designs and supports the physical and virtual infrastructure, including storage, virtualization, and network configurations.

- **Data Center Technician**: Provides on-site support for servers, cabling, and hardware within data centers. Handles physical deployments and maintenance.

Cloud Computing

Cloud computing roles focus on designing, deploying, and managing cloud-based infrastructure and services. These professionals help organizations move from traditional on-premise systems to scalable, flexible environments hosted on platforms like AWS, Azure, or Google Cloud.

Cloud specialists must understand networking, virtualization, storage, automation, and cost optimization — along with the tools needed to manage cloud workloads efficiently. These roles are in high demand as more businesses adopt cloud-first strategies.

Common roles under Cloud computing are:

- **Cloud Engineer**: Builds, configures, and manages cloud environments, often using infrastructure-as-code tools (like Terraform or CloudFormation).

- **Cloud Architect**: Designs the overall structure of cloud environments (AWS, Azure, GCP), ensuring they're scalable, secure, and cost-effective.

- **Solutions Architect (Cloud Focused)**: Works with clients or internal teams to translate business needs into cloud-based solutions and infrastructure.

- **Site Reliability Engineer (SRE)**: Ensures reliability and uptime of cloud-based applications and infrastructure using automation, monitoring, and performance tuning.

- **Cloud Security Engineer**: Protects cloud workloads, implements identity and access controls, encryption, and compliance best practices.

Automation and DevOps

Automation and DevOps roles focus on improving the speed, consistency, and quality of software development and IT operations. These professionals automate repetitive tasks, manage deployment pipelines, and bridge the gap between development and infrastructure teams.

This area requires strong knowledge of scripting, tooling, systems integration, and cloud environments. DevOps roles are especially valuable in organizations practicing agile methodologies, continuous integration, and continuous delivery (CI/CD).

Common roles under Automation and DevOps are:

- **DevOps Engineer**: Automates the software development lifecycle using CI/CD pipelines, infrastructure-as-code tools, and monitoring systems. Works closely with developers and system admins to ensure smooth deployments and scalable environments.

- **CI/CD Engineer / Build and Release Engineer**: Designs, implements, and maintains continuous integration and delivery pipelines. Works with tools like Jenkins, GitLab CI, GitHub Actions, or Azure DevOps to automate code testing and deployment.

- **Monitoring Engineer / Observability Specialist**: Sets up system and application monitoring and focuses on metrics, logs, and alerts to catch issues early and improve system health.

Cybersecurity

Cybersecurity professionals protect systems, networks, data, and users from digital threats. These roles are critical in identifying vulnerabilities, responding to incidents, and ensuring compliance with security policies and regulations.

Cybersecurity spans a wide range of responsibilities — from monitoring activity and analyzing risk to performing penetration tests and developing defensive architecture. These roles are in high demand across all industries as threats become more sophisticated and regulatory requirements increase.

Common roles under Cybersecurity are:

- **Security Analyst / SOC Analyst**: Monitors security systems, analyzes alerts, and responds to incidents. Often works in a Security Operations Center (SOC) as a first line of defense.

- **Security Engineer**: Builds and maintains the tools, systems, and practices that protect infrastructure. Works on firewalls, endpoint protection, and secure network design.

- **Security Architect**: Designs secure systems from the ground up. Focuses on integrating security principles into IT architecture and ensuring compliance with best practices.

- **Penetration Tester / Ethical Hacker**: Simulates cyberattacks to test application, network, and system vulnerabilities. Helps organizations find and fix weaknesses before attackers do.

- **GRC Analyst / Risk Analyst**: Focuses on Governance, Risk, and Compliance. Ensures that the security policies align with laws, regulations, and internal standards.

- **Security Awareness Specialist**: Develops programs to train employees on cybersecurity best practices and reduce human error-related risks.

System Architecture

System architecture professionals are responsible for designing the high-level structure of IT systems. They decide how different technologies, platforms, databases, and services fit together to support business goals at scale.

Common roles under System Architecture are:

- **Solutions Architect**: Designs complete technical solutions that align with business goals. Bridges the gap between high-level business needs and practical technical implementation.

- **Enterprise Architect**: Defines the long-term IT strategy for an organization. Focuses on aligning systems, platforms, and processes with business objectives at scale — often managing multiple projects and platforms across departments.

- **Systems Architect / Technical Architect**: Plans and documents how systems will be built — including frameworks, databases, APIs, and infrastructure. Works closely with development and infrastructure teams to ensure the system is scalable, maintainable, and secure.

The following table outlines IT Job categories, common roles, and typical experience levels, giving a snapshot of the field and career paths:

S.No.	Job Category	Common Roles	Experience Level
1.	Support and Operations	Help Desk, Desktop Support, IT Operations	Entry level
2.	Quality Assurance and Testing	QA Tester, QA Automation, Test Manager	Entry to Mid-level
3.	Non-Coding Tech Roles	Project Manager, Product Manager, Business Analyst, Scrum Master	Entry to Mid-level
4.	Software and Web Development	Frontend Dev, Backend Dev, Full Stack Dev, Software Engineer, UI/UX Designer	Entry to Mid-level
5.	Data Management and Analytics	Data Analyst, SQL Dev, Data Engineer, Data Scientist	Mid-level to Advanced
6.	AI and Machine Learning	ML Engineer, Data Scientist, NLP Engineer	Mid-level to Advanced
7.	Infrastructure and System Management	System Admin, Network Admin, Infra Engineer, IT Operations Specialist	Mid-level to Advanced
8.	Cloud Computing	Cloud Engineer, Cloud Architect, Cloud Security Eng.	Mid-level to Advanced
9.	Automation and DevOps	DevOps Engineer, SRE, CI/CD Engineer	Mid-level to Advanced
10.	Cybersecurity	Security Analyst, Pen Tester, Security Architect, GRC Analyst	Mid-level to Advanced
11.	System Architecture	Solutions Architect, Enterprise Architect, Integration Architect	Advanced to Expert

Table 2.2: Job Categories, Common Roles, and Experience Levels

Conclusion

Understanding the IT landscape is essential for building a long-term, fulfilling career in tech. This chapter outlined how the field is structured, the functions that keep it running, and the diverse career paths available — from support and operations to architecture and strategy.

Each category offers a unique mix of responsibilities, required skills, and experience levels. While some roles provide accessible entry points for newcomers, others offer deep specialization and leadership opportunities. Recognizing these distinctions helps align individual interests and capabilities with realistic and rewarding career tracks.

In the next chapter, we'll explore where these roles show up in the real world — from startups to global enterprises — and the trends shaping the future of IT work.

Frequently Asked Questions

1. What exactly does "Information Technology" include?

Ans. IT covers a wide range of technologies and roles — from hardware, networking, and security to software, data, and cloud infrastructure. It's the system of people, tools, and processes that keep digital operations running.

2. How is IT different from computer science?

Ans. Computer science focuses more on theory, algorithms, and programming. IT is practical and operational — it's about using and supporting tech in real-world environments.

3. What are the major job categories in IT?

Ans. The main categories include Support and Infrastructure, Networking, Cybersecurity, Cloud, Data/Analytics, Software Development, and Project/Tech Management. Each has its own tools, roles, and career tracks.

4. Do all IT jobs involve coding?

Ans. No. Many IT roles are focused on support, systems, data handling, user experience, or management, not coding. While programming can be useful, it's not required for every path.

5. What industries rely most on IT?

Ans. All industries use IT but finance, healthcare, education, logistics, and retail are especially tech-reliant. Each sector applies IT differently, based on its needs.

6. What's the difference between technical and non-technical roles in IT?

Ans. Technical roles involve hands-on configuration, development, or system maintenance. Non-technical roles focus more on planning, communication, analysis, or support. Both are valuable and often overlap.

7. Is it better to specialize early or stay general?

Ans. In the beginning, it's smart to explore broadly. Once you identify a track you enjoy and align with, you can specialize in it. IT careers grow through both breadth and depth — timing matters.

Quick Checklist

Use this checklist to review your progress and track what you've done. Check off each item as you complete it.

- ☐ I understand what Information Technology (IT) includes and how it differs from computer science.

- ☐ I can describe the major job categories in IT and the types of roles within each.

- ☐ I've learned that not all IT roles require coding.

- ☐ I know how IT supports different industries (for example, finance, healthcare, and retail).

- ☐ I understand the difference between working in a tech company and a non-tech company's IT department.

- ☐ I know the pros and cons of working at startups, mid-sized companies, and large enterprises.

- ☐ I've reviewed how trends like cloud, automation, and cybersecurity impact IT job demand.

- ☐ I've considered which industries align with my values or goals for a possible IT career.

- ☐ I can explain how technical and non-technical IT roles differ and where I might fit.

Tip: You don't need to check every box right now. Use this list as a progress tracker, and revisit it as you move forward.

CHAPTER 3

IT Employers and Industry Trends

Introduction

As technology becomes more integral to how the world operates, opportunities in IT are expanding across every industry. But not all companies are the same, and neither are the roles they offer.

This chapter takes a closer look at the types of organizations that hire IT talent, the sectors driving innovation, and the trends reshaping the tech workforce. Whether entering the field or planning the next move, understanding where the demand is — and how it's changing — is key to making smart career decisions.

This chapter will cover the following topics:
- Types of companies that hire IT professionals
- IT across industries
- Emerging IT career trends

Types of IT Employers

IT talent is needed across nearly every industry, but the nature of the work and the environment can vary widely depending on the type of organization. Understanding the differences can help us to identify where skills will be most valued and what kind of work culture to expect.

Tech Companies

Tech companies are companies whose core products or services are technology-based, such as software firms, app developers, SaaS providers, cloud platforms, and so on. In these companies:

- Roles are highly technical, often fast-paced, and product-driven.
- Teams may be agile, remote-friendly, and innovation-focused.

Large Enterprises

Banks, insurance companies, hospitals, retailers, and manufacturers all heavily depend on IT — even if they aren't in the tech sector. In such enterprises:

- IT teams are large, structured, and often have specialized departments (for example, networking, security, and QA).
- Offers job stability, benefits, and opportunities to grow within a company.

Startups

Smaller, fast-growing companies often focus on a single product or idea. These startup companies usually:

- Expect a fast pace, smaller teams, and more generalist roles (doing a bit of everything).
- Great for gaining wide exposure quickly, but may come with less structure.

Consulting Firms and System Integrators

Consulting firms provide outsourced IT services, custom development, or integration projects for clients. In these firms:

- Consultants work across many industries and systems.
- Strong client-facing skills are essential; work may involve frequent travel or remote delivery.

Governments and Nonprofit Organizations

Public sector and mission-driven organizations rely on secure, scalable systems — and the IT professionals who manage them. These workplaces often offer stability, structured processes, and a focus on compliance. They tend to appeal to those who prioritize long-term careers and meaningful impact over fast-paced environments or profit-driven goals.

Each type of employer offers a different experience, pace, and set of expectations. Whether someone thrives in a structured enterprise, a fast-moving startup, or a client-facing consulting role depends on personal strengths, work style, and career goals. Understanding these environments helps us make more intentional choices about where to start — or where to grow — in the IT field.

IT across Industries

Information Technology is no longer confined to tech companies; it powers every major industry. But how IT is applied can vary dramatically depending on the sector.
In some industries, the focus is on real-time systems and uptime. In others, it's compliance, automation, or user experience. Understanding these differences helps IT professionals align their skills and career choices with industries that match their interests, values, or goals.

Here's a breakdown of how IT drives value across key sectors.

Finance and Banking

The finance sector relies heavily on technology to maintain trust, security, and speed. IT systems here must handle massive transaction volumes with minimal downtime while complying with strict regulations.

IT plays a key role in supporting secure transactions, fraud detection, trading platforms, and mobile banking.

Common roles in this industry include cybersecurity specialists, data engineers, DevOps professionals, and cloud architects. It's a high-pressure, tightly regulated environment where both performance and compliance are critical.

Healthcare

Healthcare organizations depend on IT to manage sensitive patient data, enable digital diagnostics, and power telehealth services.

In healthcare, privacy, security, and accuracy are essential. IT supports electronic health record (EHR) systems, digital diagnostics, telemedicine, and patient data analysis.

Privacy requirements and regulatory compliance, such as HIPAA, play a major role in how these systems are designed and maintained. Roles in this space often combine technical expertise with domain-specific knowledge, such as clinical informatics.

Retail and E-commerce

IT drives both the customer experience and backend logistics in retail. From personalized recommendations to seamless checkout and inventory tracking, technology keeps everything connected.

It supports real-time inventory management, customer data analytics, personalized shopping experiences, and logistics. Performance at scale is essential, especially during high-traffic periods like holiday sales.

Key roles in this sector include DevOps specialists, frontend and backend developers, and experts in AI-based recommendation systems.

Artificial Intelligence in Industry

AI and machine learning are being adopted across sectors to solve complex problems and improve decision-making. In finance, they power fraud detection and algorithmic trading.

In healthcare, they assist in diagnostics and personalized treatment. In retail, AI personalizes customer journeys and optimizes inventory.

As AI continues to evolve, demand for professionals who can develop, train, and deploy intelligent systems is increasing, particularly in roles like machine learning engineer, NLP specialist, and AI researcher.

Education and EdTech

The shift toward online and hybrid learning has made IT essential in education. Learning management systems, virtual classrooms, and content delivery platforms are now standard tools.

IT supports online classrooms, digital assessments, and remote collaboration technologies. Professionals such as developers, LMS administrators, instructional designers, and infrastructure specialists play key roles in enabling these systems.

This is a sector with growing demand, driven by global changes in how education is delivered.

Manufacturing and Supply Chain

Modern manufacturing depends on connected systems and real-time data. IT supports automation, IoT integration, and predictive analytics to keep production efficient and smart.

It enables smart factories, IoT systems, real-time tracking, and predictive maintenance. Roles such as automation engineers, data analysts, and integration specialists are critical in this environment.

These systems often run 24/7 and rely on robust monitoring and control frameworks to ensure reliability and uptime.

Government and Public Sector

Government agencies use IT to provide public services, manage infrastructure, and maintain national security. Projects are often long-term, complex, and focused on accessibility and resilience. IT supports citizen services, digital IDs, secure portals, and national infrastructure. There is a strong emphasis on cybersecurity, scalability, and modernizing legacy systems. The work prioritizes long-term impact, public access, and adherence to regulatory frameworks. While many IT roles and technologies overlap across industries, each sector tends to focus on different priorities — whether it's compliance, performance, user experience, or innovation.

Emerging IT Trends

The IT field is constantly evolving — not just in terms of tools and platforms, but in how teams are structured, what employers expect, and which skills actually open doors. For anyone building a long-term career in tech, staying in sync with these shifts is essential.

The following are the most significant trends reshaping IT roles and creating new opportunities across the industry.

Cloud and Remote Infrastructure

More organizations are transitioning from on-premise systems to cloud-native architectures. This shift goes beyond hosting; it affects how systems are designed, deployed, and managed.

- Skills in platforms like AWS, Azure, and Google Cloud are now foundational.
- Infrastructure automation, remote monitoring, and containerization (for example, Docker, Kubernetes) are increasingly part of core IT functions.
- Roles like Cloud Engineer, DevOps Specialist, and Site Reliability Engineer (SRE) continue to grow.

Cybersecurity as a Core Priority

Security is now embedded into every stage of technology — from design to deployment. As threats become more sophisticated, organizations are embedding cybersecurity into infrastructure, applications, and user training.

- Demand is rising for roles like Security Analyst, Security Engineer, and Security Architect.
- Companies are looking for professionals who understand not just threat detection but secure coding, identity management, and incident response.

The Rise of Software and Web Development

Software is no longer just a product — it's how businesses operate, communicate, and grow. As a result, development roles continue to expand across all industries.

- Frontend, backend, and full-stack developers are in steady demand.

- Frameworks like React, Angular, Node.js, and Python-based stacks are widely used.
- Teams are increasingly adopting agile and DevOps practices, blurring the line between coding and deployment.

AI, Automation, and Intelligent Systems

Artificial intelligence and automation are transforming tasks across IT — not just merely replacing work, but enhancing it. From chatbots and predictive maintenance to intelligent monitoring systems, automation is becoming a standard expectation.

- IT roles now often require scripting, process automation (for example, PowerShell, Python, Ansible), or familiarity with AI-enabled tools.
- QA testers, support engineers, and even business analysts are leveraging automation to increase efficiency and accuracy.

Data Analytics, Visualization, and Reporting

Data isn't just for data scientists anymore. Everyone — from system admins to product managers — is expected to work with data in some form. And companies want actionable insights, not just raw numbers.

- Roles like Data Analyst, BI Developer, and Reporting Specialist are growing fast.
- Skills in SQL, Excel, Power BI, and tools like Tableau or Looker are becoming essential in both tech and non-tech teams.
- There's a growing emphasis on storytelling with data — making information clear, visual, and decision-ready.

Cross-functional Technologists with Business Awareness

Today's IT professionals are expected to collaborate across functions, speak the language of both users and executives, and connect technical solutions to business outcomes.

- Roles like Product Manager, Solutions Architect, and Business Analyst emphasize communication, strategic thinking, and adaptability.
- Employers increasingly value soft skills — especially in roles that involve stakeholder interaction, documentation, or end-user support.

While many IT roles and technologies overlap across industries, each sector tends to prioritize different goals — whether it's compliance, performance, user experience, or innovation. Technologies like AI and machine learning are increasingly enhancing all of them — driving efficiency, smarter decision-making, and more personalized solutions.

Conclusion

The IT field isn't just growing — it's evolving. As businesses adopt cloud, automation, AI, and data-driven decision-making, the expectations placed on IT professionals are shifting. Technical skills remain essential, but adaptability, collaboration, and business awareness are becoming crucial.

Staying ahead means keeping an eye on these trends and intentionally developing the skills that align with where the industry is going — not just where it's been.

In the upcoming chapter, we'll shift from exploring the industry to helping you choose your path — mapping out key IT tracks based on interests, strengths, and long-term goals.

Frequently Asked Questions

1. What kinds of companies hire IT professionals?

Ans. Almost every industry hires IT talent — from tech companies and banks to hospitals, schools, and retailers. Some companies have large in-house IT teams, while others outsource or rely on consultants.

2. Is it better to work in a tech company or a non-tech company's IT department?

Ans. Both have advantages. Tech companies may offer faster-paced innovation and technical depth. Non-tech companies often offer more stability, broader roles, and exposure to how tech supports business functions.

3. How do startups, mid-size companies, and large enterprises differ in IT roles?

Ans. Startups often require you to wear many hats. Mid-size firms offer specialization and growth. Large enterprises usually have structured roles and formal career paths. Your fit depends on your goals and personality.

4. Are remote IT jobs common now?

Ans. Yes. Many IT roles — especially in development, support, analytics, and cloud — are remote-friendly. However, on-site roles still exist, especially in support and security-sensitive industries.

5. How do industry trends affect job opportunities?

Ans. Trends like cloud adoption, cybersecurity, automation, and artificial intelligence shift the demand for specific skills. Staying informed about these changes helps you focus on areas with long-term relevance and strong hiring potential.

6. Should I choose an industry first or a tech skill first?

Ans. Start by building core skills in a tech domain (for example, support, data, cloud), then consider which industries align with your values or interests. Skills often transfer across industries.

7. Are certifications more important in some industries than others?

Ans. Yes. Certifications tend to carry more weight in regulated industries like government, healthcare, and finance. In contrast, startups or smaller companies may prioritize proven skills, hands-on experience, and portfolios over formal credentials.

Quick Checklist

Use this checklist to review your progress and track what you've done. Check off each item as you complete it.

☐ I can identify the types of companies that hire IT professionals.

☐ I understand the difference between tech companies and non-tech companies with internal IT roles.

☐ I've learned how company size (startup, mid-size, enterprise) affects IT roles and responsibilities.

☐ I know how remote work fits into the current IT job landscape.

☐ I understand how trends like cloud, AI, and automation influence IT hiring and skill demand.

☐ I've thought about which types of companies or industries best match my goals and preferences.

☐ I can explain how different industries apply IT in ways that affect tools, roles, and priorities.

☐ I've considered whether certifications are more important in regulated industries versus others.

Tip: *You don't need to check every box right now. Use this list as a progress tracker, and revisit it as you move forward.*

CHAPTER 4
Career Paths in IT

Introduction

Choosing a direction in IT isn't about finding the one "correct" path — it's about identifying a practical starting point that matches your interests, strengths, and current resources. Whether entering the field for the first time or looking to pivot from another role, having a clear track helps you focus, upskill with purpose, and avoid unnecessary detours.

In this chapter, we'll explore the most common career paths in IT — what each one involves, the roles they lead to, the skills and tools you'll need, and how to start building real-world experience. From support and infrastructure to development, data, security, and more, each section gives you a practical roadmap based on where you are and where you want to go. This chapter will cover the following topics:

- Career path: Support and Operations
- Career path: Quality Assurance and Testing
- Career path: Non-coding Tech Roles
- Career path: Software and Web Development
- Career path: Data Management and Analytics
- Career path: AI and Machine Learning
- Career path: Infrastructure and System Management
- Career path: Cloud Computing
- Career path: Automation and DevOps
- Career path: Cybersecurity
- Career path: System Architecture

Career Path: Support and Operations

Support and operations roles are the backbone of IT in most organizations. They are often the first point of contact when something breaks, doesn't connect, or simply needs to function more effectively. It's one of the most accessible starting points in tech — ideal for building real-world experience, learning troubleshooting skills, and understanding how systems function day to day.

Whether you're aiming to grow into system administration, networking, or cybersecurity, this path lays the technical foundation to get there.

Common roles in this path include:

- IT Support Specialist
- Help Desk Technician
- Desktop Support Technician
- IT Operations Analyst
- NOC (Network Operations Center) Technician

To succeed in this path, focus on learning:

- Operating systems: Windows, Linux (basic admin tasks)
- Networking fundamentals: IP addressing, DNS, DHCP, firewalls
- IT support tools: Active Directory, ServiceNow, Jira, remote desktop tools
- Troubleshooting: hardware, printers, networks, user access, and connectivity
- Scripting: Basic scripting using PowerShell or Bash for automating simple tasks

Here are practical ways to get started in this career path:

- Start with the basics: IT fundamentals, Excel, and Microsoft Word — these are often used daily in support roles
- Self-learn or take training programs focused on troubleshooting, systems, and user support
- Offer help to nonprofits to build hands-on experience
- Apply for entry-level roles at MSPs, small businesses, or as tech support in non-tech companies
- Focus on communication and customer service skills — they're just as important as technical ones in this field

Career Path: Quality Assurance and Testing

Quality Assurance (QA) and testing roles focus on making sure software works the way it's supposed to — without bugs, errors, or surprises. QA professionals play a key role in delivering a stable and usable product.

This path is a great entry point into IT or software teams for those who are detail-oriented, organized, and curious about how systems behave.

Common roles in this path include:

- QA Analyst
- Manual Tester
- Test Automation Engineer
- QA Engineer
- SDET (Software Development Engineer in Test)

To succeed in this path, focus on learning:
- Basics of software development and how applications work
- Testing concepts: test cases, test plans, bug tracking, regression testing
- Manual testing techniques for web and mobile apps
- Testing tools: Jira (for tracking), Postman (for APIs), TestRail or Zephyr (for test management)
- Automation tools (once you've mastered manual): Selenium, Cypress, or Playwright
- Basic scripting or programming (Python, JavaScript, or Java) is a plus for automation roles

To begin your journey in QA and Testing:
- Self-learn or take training focused on software testing fundamentals
- Start with manual testing before diving into automation
- Practice writing test cases for everyday apps (for example, your bank app, an e-commerce site)
- Explore open-source projects or testing communities to gain experience
- Apply for junior QA or testing roles in software companies, digital agencies, or startups
- Focus on clear communication, critical thinking, and attention to detail — core strengths in QA

Career Path: Non-coding Tech Roles

Non-coding tech professionals play a critical role in planning, organizing, and delivering IT projects and products. These roles are ideal for people who enjoy structure, communication, and working across teams to get things done.

This path is especially relevant for career switchers from business, operations, or customer-facing roles.

Common roles in this path include:

- Project Coordinator / Project Manager
- Product Manager / Technical Product Manager
- Business Analyst
- Scrum Master
- Technical Writer
- Program Manager

To succeed in this path, it's helpful to learn:

- Basics of software development lifecycle (SDLC)
- Agile and Scrum methodologies (how teams work in sprints, plan releases)
- Writing user stories, gathering requirements, and documenting workflows
- Tools such as Jira, Confluence, Trello, Asana, Excel, Miro
- Stakeholder communication, meeting facilitation, and planning skills
- Optional: light exposure to wireframing or data tools (Figma, Power BI) to collaborate better with technical teams

Here's how to get started in this track:

- Learn the fundamentals of Agile, Scrum, and product/project management through online courses or certifications
- Practice writing sample user stories and creating mock project plans
- Volunteer to manage small projects or documentation for open-source teams, community groups, or side projects

- If switching from another field, highlight transferable skills: organization, communication, leadership
- Apply for entry-level roles like Junior PM, Business Analyst, or Project Coordinator to get real-world exposure

Career Path: Software and Web Development

Software and web development is one of the most in-demand and versatile paths in tech. Developers build the systems, apps, and websites that power everything from internal tools to global platforms.

This path suits people who enjoy solving problems, working with logic, and turning ideas into functional tools.

With the right skills and portfolio, this is a path that offers strong career growth, remote work options, and long-term flexibility.

Common roles in this path include:
- Frontend Developer
- Backend Developer
- Full-stack Developer
- Software Engineer
- Mobile App Developer
- Web Developer

Key skills and technologies to learn include:
- Programming fundamentals: logic, loops, conditionals, functions
- Core languages as follows:
    - Frontend: HTML, CSS, JavaScript
    - Frameworks: React, Angular, Vue

- Backend: Python, .Net, C#, Java, JavaScript (Node.js), or PHP
- Version control: Git, GitHub
- Databases: Oracle, SQL Server, PostgreSQL, MySQL, NoSQL (MongoDB)
- Web frameworks: Flask, Django, Express, Spring Boot
- APIs: REST APIs, JSON, HTTP methods
- Optional: mobile frameworks (React Native, Flutter) for app development

Here's how to get started in this track:

- Begin with free or beginner-friendly platforms (freeCodeCamp, The Odin Project, Codecademy, CS50x)
- Take structured training (online bootcamps, local institutes, or instructor-led courses) to stay focused and accountable
- Build and publish personal projects: portfolios, to-do apps, weather dashboards, blogs
- Push code to GitHub to demonstrate your progress
- Join developer communities or open-source projects to gain experience and network
- Apply for internships, freelance work, or entry-level developer roles — even contract jobs can be a great start
- Focus on building consistency in learning and coding regularly

Career Path: Data Management and Analytics

Data is at the center of decision-making in almost every business. Professionals in this path collect, clean, interpret, and visualize data to uncover insights that help teams make smarter decisions.

This path is great for people who enjoy numbers, patterns, and solving real-world problems with data.

Common roles in this path include:

- Data Analyst
- Business Intelligence (BI) Analyst
- SQL Developer
- Data Engineer
- Data Scientist
- Reporting Analyst

Success in this path requires building expertise in:

- Data fundamentals: structured versus unstructured data, data types, and databases
- Excel (advanced features, pivot tables, lookups)
- SQL: writing queries, joins, aggregations, and stored procedures
- Data visualization: Power BI, Tableau, Excel dashboards
- Scripting for analysis: Python (Pandas, NumPy)
- Optional for advanced roles: ETL tools, data warehousing, cloud platforms (BigQuery, AWS Redshift)

Developing expertise in the following areas is key to success in this path:

- Take structured training in data analytics, Excel, and SQL — either online or with a training provider
- Practice building dashboards and writing SQL queries on open datasets (for example, Kaggle, Google Data)
- Create a portfolio with real-world reports or analysis projects
- Learn how to tell stories with data, not just present numbers
- Apply for junior data analyst or reporting roles, even in non-tech companies (finance, retail, healthcare, and so on)
- Stay curious — follow business and data trends in the industries you're most interested in

Career Path: AI and Machine Learning

AI and machine learning professionals design systems that learn from data, recognize patterns, and make predictions or decisions with minimal human intervention. This path is ideal for people who enjoy solving complex problems using code, math, and logic.

It's a natural progression from data roles — many professionals begin as analysts or engineers before specializing in machine learning or AI-driven development.

Common roles in this domain include:

- Machine Learning Engineer
- Data Scientist
- AI/ML Research Assistant
- NLP Engineer (Natural Language Processing)
- Computer Vision Engineer
- Deep Learning Specialist

Recommended learning areas for developing expertise in this track:

- Programming: Python (NumPy, pandas, scikit-learn, Jupyter)
- Machine learning concepts: regression, classification, clustering
- Deep learning frameworks: TensorFlow, PyTorch
- Data preparation: cleaning, feature engineering, model evaluation
- Math foundations: linear algebra, statistics, probability
- Optional: Natural language processing, computer vision, MLOps

Initial steps to enter the AI and Machine Learning career path:

- Build a strong foundation in Python and basic data analysis
- Take structured training in machine learning (online or instructor-led)
- Practice with small ML projects using open datasets (for example, Kaggle)
- Use GitHub to share models, code, and experiments
- Learn how to explain ML models and results clearly to non-technical stakeholders
- Apply for junior ML engineer, AI intern, or research assistant roles
- Stay up to date — follow new developments in AI through blogs, newsletters, and research

Career Path: Infrastructure and System Management

This path focuses on building and maintaining the core systems that run an organization's technology — from physical servers and virtual machines to internal networks and user accounts. These roles are critical behind the scenes and form the backbone of stable IT operations.

It's a strong fit for those who enjoy structured environments, problem-solving, and keeping systems running smoothly.

Common roles in this area include:

- System Administrator
- Network Administrator
- Infrastructure Engineer
- IT Operations Specialist
- Data Center Technician
- Windows/Linux Admin

Key areas of knowledge include:

- Operating systems: Windows Server, Linux (Ubuntu, CentOS, Red Hat)
- Networking: IP addressing, DNS, DHCP, routing, switching, firewalls
- Virtualization: VMware, Hyper-V, VirtualBox
- Infrastructure monitoring tools: Nagios, Zabbix, PRTG
- Directory services and access control: Active Directory, Group Policy
- Scripting for automation: PowerShell, Bash
- Optional: cloud infrastructure basics (AWS, Azure)

To gain practical experience and break into the field:

- Take training in systems administration, networking, and virtualization, with labs to simulate real environments
- Set up your own home lab to practice managing VMs, networks, and operating systems
- Offer to help small businesses or nonprofits with basic setup or troubleshooting
- Apply for roles like IT Technician, Junior SysAdmin, or NOC Engineer
- Be prepared to support on-call or rotational shifts — especially in 24/7 environments
- Build strong habits around documentation, backups, and system hygiene

Career Path: Cloud Computing

Cloud computing roles focus on designing, deploying, and managing infrastructure and applications in virtual environments — typically on platforms like AWS, Azure, or Google Cloud. This path is all about scalability, automation, and modernizing how organizations run their systems and services.

It's an ideal path for professionals with a background in infrastructure, networking, or DevOps — or for anyone who wants to work on modern platforms that support today's digital businesses.

Common roles in this path include:

- Cloud Engineer
- Cloud Administrator
- Solutions Architect (Cloud-focused)
- Cloud Infrastructure Engineer
- Site Reliability Engineer (SRE)
- Cloud Security Engineer

Key knowledge areas for this track include:

- Core cloud services: compute, storage, networking, identity, and access
- Platform-specific tools: AWS (EC2, S3, IAM), Azure (VMs, Blob, RBAC), GCP
- Infrastructure as Code: Terraform, CloudFormation, ARM templates
- Linux and Windows administration in the cloud
- Monitoring and performance tools: CloudWatch, Azure Monitor, Stackdriver
- Optional: containers (Docker), orchestration (Kubernetes), serverless functions

Steps to begin a cloud-focused career are as follows:

- Take structured cloud computing training, ideally with access to real or simulated cloud environments
- Focus on one platform first (AWS, Azure, or GCP) and build core projects (for example, hosting a website, creating a secure network, or deploying an app)
- Use free tiers or sandboxes to practice deploying infrastructure and managing services
- Learn basic scripting or automation (PowerShell, Bash, Python)
- Apply for roles like Cloud Support Associate, Junior Cloud Engineer, or DevOps Intern to get your foot in the door
- Build a portfolio of deployed environments and document your setups clearly

Career Path: Automation and DevOps

Automation and DevOps roles are all about streamlining the software delivery process, making it faster, more reliable, and easier to manage. These professionals build systems that help teams deploy code, manage infrastructure, monitor performance, and recover quickly when things go wrong.

It's a great path for people who enjoy systems thinking, problem-solving, and working across development and infrastructure teams.

Common roles in this path include:
- DevOps Engineer
- CI/CD Engineer
- Build and Release Engineer
- Site Reliability Engineer (SRE)
- Infrastructure Automation Specialist
- Platform Engineer

To succeed in this path, it helps to build expertise in:
- Operating systems (Linux especially) and system admin basics
- Version control systems: Git, GitHub, GitLab
- CI/CD tools: Jenkins, GitHub Actions, GitLab CI, Azure DevOps
- Infrastructure as Code (IaC): Terraform, Ansible, Puppet, CloudFormation
- Containers and orchestration: Docker, Kubernetes
- Scripting: Bash, Python, or Go for automating tasks and pipelines
- Monitoring and logging tools: Prometheus, Grafana, ELK stack, Datadog

Ways to start gaining experience include:
- Take DevOps or automation-focused training — especially programs with hands-on labs and real deployment practice
- Start by automating small tasks: shell scripts, config management, or local builds
- Learn to set up a basic CI/CD pipeline using free tools
- Practice deploying simple apps in containers and managing them with Docker Compose or Kubernetes
- Apply for junior DevOps or Automation roles — or transition from sysadmin/support positions
- Build and document personal DevOps projects (for example, infrastructure setup, monitored deployment pipelines) to showcase in interviews

Career Path: Cybersecurity

Cybersecurity professionals protect systems, networks, and data from threats. This path is critical in every industry — from banking and healthcare to government and tech.

Whether it's monitoring for breaches, testing defenses, or enforcing policies, cybersecurity is a great path for detail-oriented thinkers who enjoy solving puzzles and staying ahead of risks.

Common roles in this path include:
- Security Analyst / SOC Analyst
- Security Engineer
- Penetration Tester (Ethical Hacker)
- Security Architect
- GRC Analyst (Governance, Risk and Compliance)
- Incident Response Specialist

Key skills and knowledge areas to build include:
- Networking basics: ports, protocols, firewalls, DNS, TCP/IP
- Operating system security (Windows and Linux)
- Cybersecurity fundamentals: threat types, vulnerabilities, risk management
- Tools: Wireshark, Splunk, Nessus, Metasploit
- Concepts: identity and access management (IAM), encryption, secure coding, SIEM
- Optional: cloud security, governance frameworks (NIST, ISO 27001), red vs. blue team techniques

Steps to begin building experience in this field are as follows:
- Take cybersecurity training — including hands-on labs, attack simulation, and blue team tools
- Learn to secure basic systems and detect vulnerabilities
- Use platforms such as TryHackMe, Hack The Box, or CyberSecLabs to practice ethically
- Start with junior or analyst roles that offer exposure to monitoring tools and incident handling
- Build your foundational knowledge before diving into niche areas like pen testing or cloud security
- Focus on curiosity and consistency — cybersecurity is a broad field that rewards ongoing learning

Career Path: System Architecture

System architects design the big-picture structure of IT systems — deciding how technologies fit together, how systems scale, and how they meet business needs. This is a more advanced path that blends deep technical knowledge with planning, leadership, and decision-making.

It's ideal for professionals with several years of experience who want to move into high-level design, strategy, and technical leadership.

Common roles in this path include:

- Solutions Architect
- Systems Architect
- Enterprise Architect
- Technical Architect
- Infrastructure Architect
- Integration Architect

To succeed in this path, it's important to develop skills in areas such as:

- Systems design principles: scalability, reliability, performance, security
- Architecture frameworks and patterns (for example, microservices, event-driven, layered)
- Experience with infrastructure (on-prem and cloud), networking, and security
- Tools: Lucidchart, Draw.io, Visio, modeling and documentation tools
- Deep understanding of APIs, databases, backend systems, cloud architecture
- Optional: TOGAF framework, cloud architecture certifications (AWS, Azure, GCP)

To begin a career in this area, consider the following steps:

- Take architecture-focused training (cloud architecture, enterprise design, or systems strategy) once foundational skills are in place
- Study real-world architecture case studies (available via cloud provider blogs and engineering write-ups)
- Gain experience across multiple domains: development, infrastructure, security, cloud
- Start documenting and designing systems for projects you work on — even if informally
- Transition into architect roles by first working as a senior developer, tech lead, or infrastructure lead
- Focus on communication, documentation, and aligning technical decisions with business outcomes

Conclusion

Every career in IT starts with a decision — not about where you'll end up, but where to begin. Whether it's support, development, analytics, or architecture, each path has its own learning curve, tools, and opportunities. The most important step is picking a path that aligns with your interests, building real skills, and taking consistent action.

Remember, these paths are not rigid lanes — many professionals shift between them as they grow. The key is to start with focus, learn by doing, and stay adaptable as your career evolves.

In the next chapter, we'll walk through how to build the skills needed for your chosen path — including learning methods, training formats, and the certifications that truly matter.

Frequently Asked Questions

1. What does it mean to "choose a path" in IT?

Ans. Choosing a track means identifying the general area of IT you want to specialize in, such as support, networking, cybersecurity, data, cloud, development, or management. Each path has different skills, tools, and job roles.

2. How do I know which IT track is right for me?

Ans. Start with your strengths and interests. Do you enjoy solving problems, working with data, designing solutions, or helping users? Explore sample job roles, try basic tasks, and reflect on what feels engaging, not just what's trending.

3. Can I switch paths later in my career?

Ans. Yes. Many professionals move between paths as their interests or goals evolve. For example, someone may start in support and shift into cloud or cybersecurity. Skills often overlap, making transitions possible.

4. What's the most beginner-friendly IT track?

Ans. IT Support or Operations is a common starting point because it doesn't require coding and builds foundational knowledge. Data and QA testing can also be accessible with the right mindset and curiosity.

5. Should I pick the track with the highest salary?

Ans. Salary matters, but it shouldn't be the only factor. The best track for you is one that matches your natural strengths, keeps you interested, and offers long-term growth — that's where you'll perform best and advance fastest.

6. What if I'm still unsure after reading this chapter?

Ans. That's normal. Consider doing short online courses, job shadowing, or mock projects in different career paths. Exposure will help you narrow down what fits you the best.

7. Is it bad to stay general for a while before choosing?

Ans. Not at all. In the early stage, it's okay to explore broadly. Just be intentional — avoid jumping randomly between topics. A generalist approach is fine if you're using it to discover your focus.

Quick Checklist

You can use this checklist to review your progress and track what you've done. Check off each item as you complete it.

☐ I understand what it means to choose a career path in IT.

☐ I've explored different IT career paths and the kind of work involved in each.

☐ I've reflected on my strengths, interests, and what problems I enjoy solving.

☐ I've considered whether I'm more interested in people-facing or system-facing work.

☐ I understand the common entry points for career paths like support, data, cloud, and so on.

☐ I've reviewed example job roles and tools used in the tracks that interest me.

☐ I know that it's okay to explore before choosing a path — as long as I stay focused.

☐ I've identified one or two career paths I'd like to explore more deeply.

Tip: *You don't need to check every box right now. Use this list as a progress tracker, and revisit it as you move forward.*

CHAPTER 5

Building Skills for IT Career Paths

Introduction

This chapter provides a practical roadmap for each of the main IT career paths introduced earlier. For every path, you'll find a breakdown of the key concepts to understand, the tools and technologies to focus on, and how to progress from foundational knowledge to hands-on skills. Each path is designed to guide learners from beginner-level basics to job-ready capabilities, with suggestions for long-term growth where applicable.

This chapter will cover the following topics:

- Skill path: Support and Operations
- Skill path: Quality Assurance and Testing
- Skill path: Non-coding Tech Roles
- Skill path: Software and Web Development
- Skill path: Data Management and Analytics
- Skill path: AI and Machine Learning
- Skill path: Infrastructure and System Management
- Skill path: Cloud Computing
- Skill path: Automation and DevOps
- Skill path: Cybersecurity
- Skill path: System Architecture

Skill Path: Support and Operations

Support and Operations roles are often the first entry point into IT. They focus on helping users, maintaining system functionality, and troubleshooting issues. This path is ideal for those who enjoy solving problems, interacting with people, and keeping systems running smoothly.

Common starting points for this path include:

- Starting with the basics of computer systems, operating systems (especially Windows), and common workplace applications like Microsoft Office.

- Getting comfortable with navigating system settings, managing files, and basic troubleshooting is essential.

- Once the fundamentals are clear, you can move into more technical topics like networking, user management, IT service tools, and system administration.

To succeed in support and operations roles, it's important to build foundational skills in the following areas:

- **Computer and Operating System Basics**: You should learn how computers function and get familiar with Windows features, file systems, and system settings.

- **Microsoft Office Tools**: Mastering Excel is useful for ticket tracking, reporting, and documentation. Outlook helps with communication workflows.

- **Networking Fundamentals**: You need to understand IP addresses, DNS, DHCP, and basic troubleshooting using tools like ping, tracert, and ipconfig.

- **User and Device Management**: You should learn to manage user accounts, permissions, and groups in Windows and Active Directory environments.

- **IT Service Management (ITSM)**: You should get familiar with ticketing tools like ServiceNow, Jira, or Freshservice, and understand basic incident/request workflows.
- **System Administration Basics**: You should learn about system updates, patching, device configuration, and remote support tools.
- **Help Desk Procedures**: You should understand escalation paths, SLAs (Service Level Agreements), and how to log, document, and resolve common issues.
- **Optional but Valuable Skills**: Basic scripting with PowerShell or Command Prompt, along with exposure to cloud-based support tools like the Microsoft 365 Admin Center, can provide a strong advantage.

Helpful resources for learning this skill path include:

- Instructor-led training in IT fundamentals or desktop support
- Practice labs or simulators for user/device management
- Free and paid resources on Microsoft Learn, Coursera, or LinkedIn Learning

Skill Path: Quality Assurance and Testing

Quality Assurance (QA) and Testing roles ensure that software and systems function as intended before they reach the end user. This path is well-suited for those with an eye for detail, a methodical approach to work, and an interest in understanding how things break —and how to prevent them.

Getting started in this path often involves:

- You can start by learning the basics of how software is built and tested.
- You should understand the Software Development Life Cycle (SDLC), types of testing, and how to think like a tester.
- Manual testing is typically the first step, and then you can move into automation or performance testing as you grow.

To succeed in this skill path, it's important to build foundational skills in the following areas:

- **Introduction to Software Testing**: You should understand the key QA concepts like test cases, test plans, bugs/defects, and the difference between manual and automated testing.
- **Testing Types and Methodologies**: You need to learn the differences between unit, integration, system, acceptance, regression, and exploratory testing. You need to get familiar with Agile and Waterfall development cycles.
- **Test Case Design and Execution**: You should practice writing clear test cases, executing them, and logging bugs using tools like Excel or Jira.
- **Bug Tracking Tools**: You should learn how to use Jira, Bugzilla, or TestRail to log and manage defects. Understand severity, priority, and how to reproduce issues.
- **Test Management Tools**: Try to get hands-on experience with tools like Zephyr, qTest, or TestLink to manage test plans and cycles.

- **Automation Fundamentals (optional at early stage)**: Once you're comfortable with manual testing, begin learning test automation with tools like Selenium, Postman (for API testing), or Playwright.

- **Basic Scripting (Optional)**: Learning the basics of scripting (JavaScript, Python, or Java) can help when moving into automation or API testing.

- **Performance or API Testing (Advanced, optional)**: Later on, you should learn about tools like JMeter for performance testing or Postman for API testing.

Resources that support learning in this area include:

- Instructor-led QA training programs (manual and automation)
- Hands-on projects: test sample web apps or open-source platforms
- Community forums like Ministry of Testing, Test Automation University
- Beginner-friendly tools: Selenium IDE, Postman

Skill Path: Non-coding Tech Roles

Non-coding tech roles focus on connecting technical teams with business objectives. Project managers, product managers, and business analysts play a critical role in translating ideas into action, defining requirements, and ensuring the successful delivery of tech solutions. This path is well-suited for individuals with strong communication, organization, and analytical skills.

Foundational areas to focus on include:

- You can begin with understanding how software development teams operate, particularly under Agile and Scrum frameworks.
- You should learn the basics of project workflows, stakeholder communication, and how to gather and document business requirements.

To succeed in this path, it's important to develop skills in areas such as:

- **IT Project Lifecycle and Methodologies**: You should understand Agile, Scrum, and Waterfall models. You also need to learn how projects are structured and delivered in tech environments.

- **Gain Role Clarity**: You should learn the responsibilities of each role. A Business Analyst focuses on requirements, a PM on timelines/delivery, and a Product Manager on the vision and user needs.

- **Requirements Gathering and Documentation**: You should learn to create BRDs (Business Requirements Documents), user stories, and wireframes. Understand how to translate business needs into tech requirements

- **Communication and Stakeholder Management**: You need to learn about the best practices for meeting management, updates, presentations, and aligning different teams

- **Tool Proficiency**: You need to get hands-on with tools like Jira, Confluence, Microsoft Excel, PowerPoint, Miro, and Notion. Familiarity with project tracking and documentation platforms is essential

- **Basic Technical Understanding**: You should learn the basic concepts around databases, APIs, and software testing. This helps in understanding developer and QA conversations

- **Business Intelligence Tools (Optional)**: You can learn Tableau or Power BI for roles where data storytelling is needed

The following resources can help build skills in this path:

- Structured training programs in Business Analysis, Agile, or Product Management

- Mock projects — create a requirements doc, build a wireframe, or manage a sample backlog

- Community meetups (for example, Agile user groups, PM/BA forums)

Skill Path: Software and Web Development

Software and web development is one of the most in-demand and versatile career paths in IT. Developers design, build, and maintain websites, applications, and software tools that power businesses and services. This path is ideal for those who enjoy problem-solving, logical thinking, and building things from the ground up.

Common starting points for this path include:

- Learning how the web works — understanding the relationship between browsers, servers, and code

- Then, moving into HTML, CSS, and JavaScript to build your first simple web pages

- From there, expand into programming languages, frameworks, and databases based on your interests and goals

Key concepts and tools to focus on in this area include:

- **Web Basics**: You need to learn how websites work — HTTP, frontend versus backend, and how code runs in the browser versus the server.

- **HTML, CSS, JavaScript**: These are the core front-end technologies. You should learn to create web pages, style them, and add interactivity.

- **Version Control with Git**: You need to learn about Git and GitHub for source code management, collaboration, and project tracking.

- **Front-end Frameworks**: For those who are focusing on UI, you should learn a JavaScript framework like React, Angular, or Vue to build dynamic, scalable front ends.

- **Programming Fundamentals**: Learning programming logic, variables, loops, functions, and problem-solving using languages like Java, JavaScript, or Python is essential.

- **Back-end Basics**: For full-stack or back-end developers, you need to learn server-side programming using Node.js, Python, Java, or PHP. You should also understand how APIs work

If you're unsure which language to start with for back-end development or general programming, here's a comparison between Python and Java. Both Python and Java are widely used in IT, but they suit different roles.

Here's a quick comparison to guide your focus:

Feature	Python	Java
Ease of learning	Simpler syntax, beginner-friendly	Structured and more verbose
Use cases	Data analysis, scripting, automation, AI	Enterprise apps, Android, backend systems
Community	Strong in data science and automation	Strong in large-scale engineering teams
Performance	Fast prototyping and flexibility	Faster runtime, optimized for scale
Best for	Data Analysts, ML Engineers, generalists	Software Engineers, App Developers

Table 5.1: Comparison between Python and Java

- **Databases**: You should learn to use SQL databases (like MySQL or PostgreSQL) and NoSQL options (like MongoDB).

- **Project Development**: You should build real-world applications — for example, task managers, blogs, dashboards, e-commerce sites.

- **Optional Advanced Tools**: Webpack, Docker, or CI/CD tools for deployment; Testing frameworks (Jest, Cypress); Mobile or cross-platform development (React Native, Flutter).

The following resources are useful for building skills in this path:

- FreeCodeCamp, Codecademy, MDN Web Docs for self-learners
- Structured full-stack or front-end development bootcamps
- Project-based courses that guide you in building apps
- GitHub for version control and sharing your work

Skill Path: Data Management and Analytics

Data professionals turn raw information into insights that support smarter business decisions. Whether cleaning data, analyzing trends, or visualizing performance, this track suits people who enjoy working with numbers, finding patterns, and presenting data clearly.

Getting started in this path often involves:

- Understanding how data is stored, retrieved, and structured
- You need to learn the basics of Excel and SQL — two core tools used across nearly all data roles
- Once comfortable, you can proceed with data analysis, reporting tools, and scripting

Learn the following to pursue this skill:

- **Data Fundamentals**: You need to learn about structured versus unstructured data, rows and columns, tables, and databases.
- **Excel for Analysis**: You should master formulas, pivot tables, data cleaning, filters, and charts. Excel is often the first tool used in reporting.
- **SQL (Structured Query Language)**: You need to learn how to query databases using SELECT, JOIN, GROUP BY, subqueries, and write efficient queries.
- **Data Visualization Tools**: You should learn to use tools like Tableau, Power BI, or Excel dashboards to communicate insights visually.

If you're deciding which tool to start with, here's a quick comparison between Tableau and Power BI to help you choose based on your needs and goals.

Both tools are widely used in BI roles. Here's how they compare at a glance:

Feature	Tableau	Power BI
Platform	Independent (Salesforce-owned)	Microsoft ecosystem
Ease of use	Highly flexible, more design options	User-friendly, especially for Excel users
Integration	Great with cloud databases	Seamless with other Microsoft products
Licensing	Expensive	More affordable with the Microsoft stack
Best for	Interactive dashboards with design freedom	Operational reporting and enterprise use

Table 5.2: Comparison between Tableau and Power BI

- **Scripting for Analysis**: For those proceeding into advanced roles, you need to learn Python for data analysis using libraries like Pandas and NumPy

- **ETL and Data Warehousing (Optional)**: You can also learn about extract-transform-load processes, data pipelines, and platforms like AWS Redshift or Google BigQuery

- **BI and Reporting Automation (Optional)**: You can also learn how to automate reports, build dashboards with real-time data, and connect data sources

The following resources are useful for building skills in this path:

- Courses in Excel, SQL, Power BI, or Tableau (self-paced or instructor-led)
- Practice using public datasets via Kaggle or Google Data
- Structured training programs in data analytics and visualization
- Projects such as building dashboards, analyzing business data, and publishing insights

Skill Path: AI and Machine Learning

AI and machine learning professionals build systems that can learn from data and make predictions or decisions without being explicitly programmed for every outcome. This path suits individuals who are curious, analytical, and interested in math, logic, and data-driven problem-solving.

Foundational areas to focus on include:

- Knowledge of Python, basic statistics, and data handling
- Understanding how to clean and prepare data is essential before jumping into algorithms or model training
- Building small, practical projects early will help apply abstract concepts

To succeed in this path, it's important to develop skills in areas such as:

- **Python Programming**: You should learn Python syntax, variables, functions, loops, and libraries like NumPy and Pandas for data handling.
- **Math Foundations**: You should build a base in statistics, probability, and linear algebra — these are the keys to understanding how models work.
- **Data Cleaning and Preparation**: You should learn to handle missing data, outliers, encoding, normalization, and feature engineering.
- **Machine Learning Basics**: You should understand supervised and unsupervised learning, model training, testing, and evaluation metrics.
- **ML Libraries and Tools**: You should learn to use Scikit-learn for basic models (linear regression, classification, clustering) and also practice with Jupyter Notebooks.

- **Project Building**: You need to create real-world projects such as prediction models, classification tasks, or recommendation engines, and share them on GitHub.
- **Optional Specializations**: Natural Language Processing (NLP), Computer Vision, MLOps and model deployment, and Large Language Models (LLMs) are a few optional talents to acquire.

The following resources can support skill development in this path:

- Structured ML and Python training (instructor-led or platforms like Coursera, DataCamp)
- Practice projects on Kaggle, Google Colab, Hugging Face Datasets
- AI communities and competitions
- Blogs, newsletters, and GitHub repos to stay updated

Skill Path: Infrastructure and System Management

This track focuses on maintaining and supporting the hardware, software, and networks that organizations rely on to operate. Professionals in this field manage servers, operating systems, and networks, ensuring reliability, uptime, and secure access.

Getting started in this path often involves:

- Knowledge of computer architecture, operating systems (especially Windows and Linux), and networking fundamentals
- It's important to get familiar with managing users, systems, and permissions
- Additionally, you should also practice using system admin tools and command-line interfaces

You need to learn the following to pursue this skill:

- **Hardware and Operating System Basics**: You should understand how systems run: memory, processors, disks, and the role of the OS. It is worth knowing the basics of both Windows and Linux.

- **Networking Fundamentals**: You need to learn about IP addressing, DNS, DHCP, subnets, routing, ports, and protocols. You must also practice using command-line tools like ping, tracert, and netstat.

- **User and Permission Management**: You should learn how to create, manage, and secure user accounts, roles, and groups in both local and domain environments (for example, Active Directory).

- **System Administration Tools**: You must know how to use tools like PowerShell, Remote Desktop, and system consoles to configure, update, and troubleshoot systems.

- **Server Management**: You should learn how to set up, configure, and monitor servers — file servers, application servers, print servers, and so on.

- **Patch Management and Security Practices**: You should know how to manage OS and software updates, apply security patches, and use antivirus and firewall tools.

- **Monitoring and Logging Tools**: You should learn how to monitor performance, set alerts, and troubleshoot issues using tools like Nagios, Zabbix, or built-in OS utilities.

- **Virtualization and Scripting** cer(**Optional**): Additionally, you can learn the basics of virtualization (VMware, Hyper-V) and write simple scripts for automation using PowerShell or Bash.

The following resources are commonly used to build skills in this path:

- Instructor-led courses covering system administration and networking
- Online platforms such as Microsoft Learn, Linux Academy, Cisco Networking Academy
- Hands-on labs or virtual environments to practice system setup
- Work on projects to set up a home lab, build a file server, and configure users and roles

Skill Path: Cloud Computing

Cloud computing professionals design, deploy, and manage scalable infrastructure and services on platforms like AWS, Azure, or Google Cloud. This path is ideal for those interested in virtual infrastructure, cost optimization, and building solutions that run in the cloud rather than on local servers.

Common starting points for this path include:

- Understanding of cloud computing, how it differs from traditional IT infrastructure, and the basic services offered by major cloud providers.
- Then you can move into hands-on work with virtual machines, storage, networking, and deployment models.

Learning the following topics will help build a strong foundation:

- **Cloud Fundamentals**: You should understand IaaS, PaaS, SaaS; regions and availability zones; and the shared responsibility model.

- **Introduction to Major Cloud Platforms**: You must learn the basics of AWS, Microsoft Azure, or Google Cloud — pick one platform to start. You should learn about the dashboards, service structure, and billing model.

- **Compute, Storage, and Networking Services**: You should get hands-on with virtual machines (EC2, Azure VMs), object storage (S3, Blob Storage), and networking (VPCs, subnets, gateways).

- **Identity and Access Management (IAM)**: You should learn how to create and manage users, roles, and permissions to securely control access to resources.

- **Cloud Monitoring and Cost Management**: You must use built-in tools to track usage, monitor services, and manage cloud spend efficiently.

- **Infrastructure as Code (IaC)**: You should learn to provision resources using tools like Terraform, AWS CloudFormation, or Azure Bicep.

- **Containers and Serverless (Optional)**: You should explore ECS, EKS, Lambda (AWS), Azure Functions, or GCP Cloud Run.

If you're trying to decide which cloud platform to focus on first, here's a quick comparison of AWS and Azure to help guide your choice. Both cloud platforms are widely used in IT roles.

This comparison will help you decide which one to start with:

Feature	AWS	Azure
Market Share	Largest global cloud provider	Second largest, rapidly growing
Integration	Broad services across cloud categories	Seamless with Microsoft tools (for example, Office, Windows)
Ease of Use	Steeper learning curve	Easier for those familiar with Microsoft
Certifications	Highly valued across many industries	Preferred in Microsoft-centric organizations
Best For	Cloud architects, startups, DevOps	Enterprise IT, hybrid cloud environments

Table 5.3: Comparison between AWS and Azure

The following resources can help develop the skills required for this path:

- Structured cloud training (AWS, Azure, GCP) — instructor-led or online platforms
- Cloud labs/sandboxes (AWS Free Tier, Azure for Students)
- Practice projects: deploy a website, create a secure storage bucket, build a virtual private network
- Certification prep materials and hands-on labs

Skill Path: Automation and DevOps

DevOps and automation professionals streamline the software development and deployment lifecycle. They focus on infrastructure automation, continuous integration/continuous delivery (CI/CD), monitoring, and improving system reliability. This path is a great fit for those who enjoy problem-solving, scripting, and bridging development and operations.

Getting started in this path often involves:

- Gaining a solid understanding of basic development workflows and system administration

- Learning version control (Git), basics of scripting, and how applications are built and deployed

- Then moving into CI/CD pipelines, containerization, and infrastructure as code

You need to learn the following to pursue this skill:

- **Version Control with Git**: You should learn Git fundamentals — branches, merges, pull requests — and how to collaborate via GitHub or GitLab.

- **Basic Scripting and Automation**: You must also learn scripting languages like Bash, PowerShell, or Python to automate tasks like backups, deployments, or user creation.

- **CI/CD Concepts**: You should understand the principles of continuous integration and delivery. Also, you should learn how to automate code testing, builds, and deployment pipelines.

- **Tools for CI/CD**: You need to get hands-on with tools like Jenkins or GitHub Actions to start, especially if you're using GitHub. GitLab CI is also widely used in GitOps environments.

If you're trying to decide which CI/CD tool to start with, here's a quick comparison of Jenkins and GitHub Actions to help guide your choice.

Both Jenkins and GitHub Actions are used for automating software builds, tests, and deployments. Here's how they compare:

Feature	Jenkins	GitHub Actions
Setup	Self-hosted, flexible configuration	Cloud-native, GitHub-integrated
Ease of Use	Requires setup and plugins	Simpler for GitHub users
Use Case	Custom CI/CD for enterprise and open-source	CI/CD pipelines for GitHub projects
Community	Established with broad plugin support	Rapid growth, native to GitHub
Best For	Experienced DevOps engineers	Beginners or GitHub-centric workflows

Table 5.4: Comparison between Jenkins and GitHub Actions

- **Infrastructure as Code (IaC):** You should learn how to define and provision cloud infrastructure using Terraform, Ansible, or AWS CloudFormation.

- **Containerization and Orchestration:** Learning the basics of Docker and progressing to orchestration with Kubernetes for deploying and scaling containerized applications is beneficial.

- **Monitoring and Logging:** You should use tools like Prometheus, Grafana, ELK Stack, or Cloud-native monitoring tools to track system health and logs.

- **Optional: Security and Compliance in DevOps**: You must learn the basics of DevSecOps, including secrets management, automated security checks, and role-based access.

The following resources can help develop the skills required for this path:

- DevOps-focused courses on platforms like Udemy, Pluralsight, or KodeKloud
- Instructor-led hands-on DevOps bootcamps
- Practice setting up pipelines, containerizing apps, and using IaC tools in labs or on cloud platforms
- GitHub for code versioning and project sharing

Skill Path: Cybersecurity

Cybersecurity professionals protect systems, data, and networks from threats. This path is ideal for those who are analytical, detail-oriented, and interested in identifying vulnerabilities and defending against attacks. Roles range from hands-on defense to policy, auditing, and compliance.

Foundational areas to focus on include:

- Understanding how systems, networks, and the internet work
- You can also learn the fundamentals of threats, vulnerabilities, and how to secure systems
- As you grow, specialize in areas like security operations, ethical hacking, or governance and compliance

You need to learn the following to pursue this skill:

- **Cybersecurity Fundamentals**: You must understand the key concepts, such as the CIA triad (Confidentiality, Integrity, Availability), types of attacks, firewalls, malware, authentication, and encryption.

- **Networking and Operating System Basics**: You should learn about IPs, ports, DNS, firewalls, and how operating systems (especially Windows and Linux) are structured and secured.

- **Security Tools and Techniques**: You should learn to use tools like Wireshark (network analysis), Nmap (scanning), and antivirus/firewall systems.

- **Identity and Access Management (IAM)**: You should also understand how to control user access, implement least privilege, and secure authentication processes.

- **Security Monitoring and Incident Response**: You should learn how to detect and respond to threats. Explore SIEM tools like Splunk or Microsoft Sentinel.

- **Penetration Testing and Vulnerability Scanning** (Optional, Advanced): Learning advanced concepts like Kali Linux, Metasploit, and Burp Suite for ethical hacking or red teaming is optional.

- **Security Frameworks and Governance**: You should understand standards like NIST, ISO 27001, GDPR, and security audits — especially for GRC or compliance roles.

The following resources can help develop the skills for this path:

- Structured training (Security+, CEH prep, cyber bootcamps)
- Capture The Flag (CTF) platforms, TryHackMe, Hack The Box

- Work on Projects such as setting up a secure lab, simulating attacks, and writing basic security policies
- Cybersecurity blogs, threat intel feeds, and community forums

Skill Path: System Architecture

System architects design the high-level structure of IT systems. They make decisions about how different components — software, databases, networks, and cloud services — fit together to meet business needs. This role suits professionals who enjoy big-picture thinking, strategic planning, and translating technical concepts into scalable solutions.

Common starting points for this path:

- System architecture is generally not an entry-level role.
- Most professionals begin as developers, administrators, or engineers and transition into architecture after gaining hands-on experience across systems.
- A solid starting point is to develop an understanding of how applications and infrastructure interact, then gradually build the ability to design solutions across complex systems.

You need to learn the following to pursue this skill:

- **Foundations in IT Systems**: You should develop strong skills in system administration, networking, software development, and cloud platforms.
- **System Design Principles**: You should learn how to think in terms of scalability, fault tolerance, high availability, and modular design.
- **Architecture Patterns**: You must study patterns like client-server, microservices, monolith versus distributed systems, and event-driven architecture.

- **Cloud Architecture**: You should learn to design systems on AWS, Azure, or GCP. You should also understand trade-offs between performance, cost, and reliability.

- **API Design and Integration**: You should learn how different services communicate using REST, GraphQL, message queues, and service buses.

- **Security and Compliance in Architecture**: You should learn to design with security in mind — encryption, access control, secure communications, and governance.

- **Documentation and Communication**: You must practice creating architecture diagrams, technical documentation, and business-aligned proposals.

The following resources can help build skills for this path:

- Architecture-focused instructor-led courses and cloud certification training
- Real-world case studies and whitepapers from AWS, Microsoft, and Google
- Work on hands-on projects such as designing a scalable application architecture, migration plans, or cloud deployment frameworks
- Use tools like Lucidchart, Draw.io, or Visio to build and present system designs

Conclusion

Choosing a career path is just the beginning — mastering the skills that power it takes focus, structure, and continuous learning. Each path in IT has its own learning curve, tools, and progression, but all offer growth opportunities with the right preparation and mindset. Whether starting in support, building toward architecture, or diving into AI, following a structured skill path helps us to turn interest into capability and capability into confidence.

In the next chapter, we'll explore how to build those skills, including effective learning formats, practical training methods, and certifications that carry real value in today's job market.

Frequently Asked Questions

1. What's the difference between a career path and a skill path?

Ans. A career path is the general direction or role type you choose in IT (for example, support, data, cloud). A skill path is the sequence of tools, technologies, and learning steps that help you succeed in that role. Career path = destination; skill path = roadmap.

2. How do I know which skills to prioritize for my chosen track?

Ans. You must start with the core tools and concepts used daily in that track. For example, in support roles, learn ticketing systems and troubleshooting. In data, focus on Excel, SQL, and BI tools. You must follow a roadmap or beginner-friendly learning path to stay on track.

3. Can I learn multiple tracks at once?

Ans. It's possible, but not recommended. You should focus on one track first — get comfortable with the basics, build confidence, and then expand. Jumping between tracks early can slow your progress and confuse.

4. Do I need certifications for every skill path?

Ans. No. Certifications can help validate skills, but they're not always required. Employers value practical experience, portfolios, and a clear understanding. You should use certifications as a supplement, not a substitute, for hands-on learning.

5. What's the best way to learn the skills in a path?

Ans. Combine structured learning (courses, bootcamps) with hands-on practice. You must follow one learning format at a time. You can use tutorials, build projects, and apply what you learn in real or simulated environments.

6. How long does it take to complete a skill path?

Ans. It varies by track and time commitment. A focused learner can gain beginner-level skills in 8–12 weeks. Mastery takes longer, but you don't need to know everything before applying for entry-level roles.

7. What if I'm overwhelmed by the number of tools in a skill path?

Ans. Prioritize the top 2–3 tools that are most used in that role. Learn them well before adding more. Skill paths are designed to be followed step-by-step, not all at once.

Quick Checklist

You can use this checklist to review your progress and track what you've done. Check off each item as you complete it:

☐ I understand the difference between a career path and a

skill path.

☐ I've identified the skills required for my chosen IT track.

☐ I know which tools and technologies are most relevant in my track.

☐ I've explored learning paths or roadmaps that match my career goals.

☐ I've prioritized a few key tools or topics to focus on first.

☐ I've started a project or exercise to apply skills in a real-world context.

☐ I understand that I don't need to master every tool to move forward.

☐ I've committed to focusing on one track at a time before branching out.

Tip: *You don't need to check every box right now. Use this list as a progress tracker, and revisit it as you move forward.*

CHAPTER 6

Learning Methods and Certifications

Introduction

Today, there are numerous methods to acquire IT skills, but not all of them yield results. The format, structure, and credibility of what's learned can make a real difference in how quickly skills translate into confidence and career progress.

This chapter explores practical learning formats and certifications that matter, helping learners make smart choices based on their goals, time, and stage in the journey.

This chapter will cover the following topics:

- Learning options: what works and why
- Certifications that matter

Learning Options: What Works and Why

While the number of ways to learn IT skills has exploded — from online platforms to immersive bootcamps — not all methods are equally effective. Real progress depends on choosing options that provide structure, relevance, and hands-on experience, not just information. Choosing the right learning format can save you time, keep you motivated, and help you apply what you're learning faster.

Here's a breakdown of the most common options and how to choose what works for your situation.

Self-paced Learning (Online Courses, YouTube, and Blogs)

This method is the best for motivated learners who prefer flexibility and low cost. It allows learners to set their own pace and explore topics freely. It is also ideal for gaining initial exposure or supplementing other forms of training. However, without structure, it's easy to become overwhelmed or lose consistency.

Instructor-led or Structured Training

This method is the best for learners who want accountability, guidance, and a clear path to job readiness. It provides a defined path to skill development with clear learning objectives. It often includes support, feedback, and access to instructors or mentors.

This method is particularly effective for individuals transitioning careers or pursuing certifications. Instructor-led virtual training offers the same real-time interaction, feedback, and structure as in-person classes — but with added flexibility, no commute, and the convenience of learning from anywhere.

Note: For those pursuing a career change or preparing for certification, structured training often leads to faster, more reliable results than self-directed learning.

Bootcamps (Online or In-Person)

This method is the best for learners who want an immersive experience and can commit full-time. Bootcamps are fast-paced and intense, often lasting 8 to 16 weeks. They cover job-ready skills and usually include portfolio projects.

Some are expensive and not all deliver on job placement promises, so research carefully.

Community Colleges or University Programs

This method is the best for learners who prefer a formal classroom environment or want credits/degrees. It is slower-paced and more academic in nature.

It may include general education courses that aren't directly job-related. It is better suited for long-term learners or those combining education with part-time work.

Next, we will discuss how to choose our work format, which is as follows:

- For structure and support: instructor-led or structured training is often most effective.

- For flexibility: a combination of self-paced resources with clear milestones works well.

- For experienced professionals: targeted, Instructor-led, or self-guided learning can close specific skill gaps.

- For beginners: foundational training with a guided curriculum can reduce the learning curve.

No single learning method works for everyone. The most effective approach depends on the learner's goals, schedule, and preferred learning style. Whether through structured training, hands-on bootcamps, or flexible self-paced courses, the key is to stay consistent and choose a path that leads to real understanding — not just completion.

Choosing a Learning Format

Each learning format has its strengths. Here's a side-by-side comparison to help you choose what fits best:

Feature	Self-Paced	Instructor-Led	Bootcamp	College Degree
Flexibility	Maximum flexibility	Fixed schedule	Intensive and fixed	Semester-based
Support	Minimal (forums, email)	Live interaction with instructors	Live instruction + mentoring	Professors, advisors
Structure	DIY learning path	Structured curriculum	Highly structured	Accredited curriculum
Pace	Go at your own pace	Moderate, paced by instructor	Fast-tracked	Slow, over 2–4 years
Cost	Often low/free	Moderate	High	Very high
Credentials	Certificates of completion	Training certificates	Bootcamp certificate	Degree
Best For	Self-motivated learners	Those needing guidance	Career switchers with time	Students seeking full credentials

Table 6.1: Comparison between different learning formats

Certifications That Matter

Certifications can open doors in IT — but only when used strategically. Not all certifications carry weight in the job market, and collecting them without building real-world skills rarely leads to results.

In some tracks, like support, cloud, and cybersecurity, certifications are often required or expected. In other areas, such as web development or AI/ML, portfolios and real-world projects often matter more than a certificate.

Choose certifications that align with your career path and skill level. Start with foundational ones and move to role-specific or advanced certifications once you gain experience.

This section highlights certifications that align with actual roles and learning paths, helping learners choose credentials that are worth the time and investment.

These certifications are useful to:

- Serve as proof of skills for those without prior IT experience
- Help career switchers validate new knowledge
- Strengthen a resume in competitive or specialized fields (for example, cloud, security)
- Sometimes required by employers, especially in government or regulated industries

Next, let's see when these Certifications are not helpful:

- Used as a substitute for hands-on experience or project work
- Chosen based on popularity, not relevance to the desired role
- Earned without understanding the underlying concepts

Role-relevant Certifications

The following is a breakdown of certifications aligned with major IT career tracks. Each certification mentioned is recognized by employers and provides structured learning to help professionals validate their skills. These are organized by track and include a brief explanation of what each certification covers and who provides it.

Recommended Certifications for Support and Operations

For those pursuing a career in IT support or operations, the following entry-level certifications provide strong foundational knowledge and are widely recognized by employers across the industry:

- **Google IT Support Professional Certificate** (*offered by Coursera/Google*): This is a beginner-friendly certification that covers IT fundamentals, troubleshooting, networking, and system administration. It is ideal for those starting in help desk or tech support roles.

- **Microsoft Certified: Azure Fundamentals** (*offered by Microsoft*): This certification introduces core cloud services and Azure concepts. It is helpful for support roles in organizations using Microsoft-based cloud environments.

- **AWS Certified Cloud Practitioner** (*offered by Amazon Web Services*): This certification covers cloud basics and how AWS services are used in business environments. It is useful for understanding cloud-connected systems in support roles.

- **CompTIA A+** (*offered by CompTIA*): This is a widely accepted foundational certification covering hardware, software, networking, and troubleshooting. It is commonly required for desktop support and technician positions.

- **Microsoft 365 Certified: Fundamentals** (*offered by Microsoft*): This certification focuses on the basics of Microsoft 365 services, including Teams, Exchange, and SharePoint. All these are important tools in modern IT support environments.

- **ITIL Foundation** (*offered by AXELOS*): This certification introduces IT service management (ITSM) principles. It is valuable for support professionals working in environments with formal service processes.

Recommended certifications for Quality Assurance and Testing

For those starting in software testing, these certifications help build credibility, reinforce core testing concepts, and provide a structured path into both manual and automated testing roles:

- **ISTQB Foundation Level** (*offered by International Software Testing Qualifications Board*): This is the most recognized entry-level certification in QA, covering software testing principles, test design techniques, and lifecycle management.

- **Certified Selenium Tester Foundation** (*offered by iSQI*): This certification focuses on browser-based automation using Selenium WebDriver. It is ideal for testers transitioning to automation.

Recommended Certifications for Non-coding Tech Roles

For roles like project management, business analysis, and team facilitation, these certifications establish foundational knowledge and signal credibility in both technical and cross-functional environments:

- **Certified Scrum Master (CSM)** (*offered by Scrum Alliance*): This certification covers Agile methodology and the Scrum framework. It is commonly pursued by Project Managers, Scrum Masters, and team leads in IT.

- **PMI-CAPM (Certified Associate in Project Management)** (*offered by Project Management Institute*): This is a globally recognized certification that validates knowledge of project management principles.

- **ECBA (Entry Certificate in Business Analysis)** (*offered by IIBA*): This certification is ideal for those starting in business analysis. It covers the basics of stakeholder management, requirements gathering, and business processes.

- **CBAP (Certified Business Analyst Professional)** (*offered by IIBA*): This is an advanced certification for experienced business analysts. It validates expertise in business analysis planning, requirements management, and solution evaluation.

Recommended Certifications for Software and Web Development

While certifications can help signal technical ability, employers in this field place a high value on portfolios and real-world projects. Building and showcasing personal or collaborative projects is often more impactful than certification alone.

Some certifications under this category are as follows:

- **Oracle Certified Professional: Java SE / Java EE** (*offered by Oracle*): This certification validates Java programming expertise, often required for backend or enterprise application development.

- **Meta Front-End Developer Professional Certificate** (*offered by Coursera/Meta*): This certification covers HTML, CSS, JavaScript, and React, along with tools like GitHub and VS Code. It is designed to help learners build and deploy responsive websites.

- **Meta Back-End Developer Professional Certificate** (*offered by Coursera/Meta*): This certification focuses on databases, APIs, server-side development with Python, and deployment best practices. It is useful for aspiring backend developers.

- **freeCodeCamp Certifications** (*offered by freeCodeCamp.org*): They offer comprehensive, project-based certifications in responsive web design, JavaScript algorithms, front-end libraries, APIs, and more — all free and open-source.

Recommended certifications for Data Management and Analytics

For those pursuing careers in data analysis, visualization, or engineering, certifications can help validate technical proficiency and familiarity with widely used tools. The following credentials are especially helpful for beginners or early-career professionals:

- **Google Data Analytics Professional Certificate** (*offered by Coursera/Google*): This certification covers data cleaning, analysis, visualization, and tools like SQL and spreadsheets. It is designed for beginners.

- **Microsoft Certified: Data Analyst Associate** (*offered by Microsoft*): This certification focuses on using Power BI to model, visualize, and analyze data.

- **Tableau Desktop Specialist** (*offered by Tableau*): This certification demonstrates basic skills in Tableau for visual analytics and dashboard building.

- **IBM Data Science Professional Certificate** (*offered by Coursera/IBM*): This certification covers core data science and machine learning skills, including Python, SQL, Pandas, and data visualization tools.

- **Microsoft Certified: Azure Enterprise Data Analyst Associate** (*offered by Microsoft*): This certification is geared toward professionals working with large-scale data models, ETL pipelines, and enterprise BI solutions.

- **Oracle Database SQL Certified Associate** (*offered by Oracle*): This certification validates foundational skills in writing SQL queries and managing relational databases using Oracle Database.

- **AWS Certified Data Analytics – Specialty** (*offered by AWS*): This certification focuses on using AWS services for data lakes, analytics pipelines, and business intelligence. It is ideal for cloud-based data analytics professionals.

Recommended Certifications for AI and Machine Learning

As AI technologies continue to grow in importance, certifications can help demonstrate specialized knowledge in machine learning models, tools, and cloud-based AI services. These credentials are particularly useful for professionals looking to stand out in technical ML roles:

- **AWS Certified Machine Learning – Specialty** *(offered by Amazon Web Services)*: This certification validates skills in designing, implementing, and maintaining ML solutions on the AWS cloud.

- **Microsoft Certified: Azure AI Engineer Associate** *(offered by Microsoft):* This certification focuses on building and managing AI solutions within Microsoft Azure.

- **Google Cloud Certified - Machine Learning Engineer** *(offered by Google Cloud)*: This certification validates skills in building and maintaining models within Google Cloud.

- **Certified Artificial Intelligence Consultant (CAIC™)** *(offered by Global Tech Council)*: This is a globally recognized certification for AI/ML professionals.

- **AWS Certified AI Practitioner** *(offered by Amazon Web Services)*: This certification validates understanding of AI, ML, and generative AI concepts on AWS.

- **IBM AI Engineering Professional Certificate** *(offered by IBM via Coursera)*: This certification covers deep learning, NLP, and AI development.

- **Professional Certificate in Machine Learning and Artificial Intelligence (UC Berkeley and MIT)** *(offered by UC Berkeley and MIT)*: This certification provides a comprehensive foundation in ML/AI and practical skills.

Recommended Certifications for Infrastructure and System Management

For professionals managing on-premise, cloud, or hybrid IT environments, the following certifications validate critical infrastructure and systems expertise:

- **Microsoft Certified: Windows Server Hybrid Administrator Associate** (*offered by Microsoft*): This certification covers on-premises, hybrid, and cloud infrastructure management with Windows Server and Azure.

- **Red Hat Certified System Administrator (RHCSA)** (*(offered by Red Hat*): This certification focuses on Linux system management, including file systems, networking, and user permissions.

- **Cisco Certified Network Associate (CCNA)** (*offered by Cisco*): This certification is recognized for foundational networking knowledge, often required in networking and infrastructure roles.

Recommended Certifications for Cloud Computing

Cloud certifications demonstrate expertise in designing, deploying, and managing services across major cloud platforms. The following are widely recognized and valued by employers:

- **AWS Certified Solutions Architect – Associate** (*offered by Amazon Web Services*): This certification covers the design of cloud environments using AWS services. It is one of the most sought-after cloud certifications.

- **Microsoft Certified: Azure Administrator Associate** (*offered by Microsoft*): This certification focuses on managing Azure resources, including networking, storage, compute, and identity.

- **Google Associate Cloud Engineer** (*offered by Google Cloud*): This certification validates the ability to deploy and manage Google Cloud-based applications.

Recommended Certifications for Automation and DevOps

Certifications in this area validate skills in automating infrastructure, managing CI/CD pipelines, and streamlining deployment processes. The following are highly regarded in the DevOps space:

- **HashiCorp Certified: Terraform Associate** (*offered by HashiCorp*): This certification focuses on infrastructure-as-code and using Terraform to automate cloud provisioning.
- **AWS Certified DevOps Engineer – Professional** (*offered by Amazon Web Services*): This is a more advanced certification covering CI/CD, automation, monitoring, and security in AWS environments.
- **Certified Kubernetes Administrator (CKA)** (*offered by Linux Foundation*): This certification validates skills in deploying, scaling, and managing Kubernetes clusters.

Recommended Certifications for Cybersecurity

Cybersecurity certifications help validate expertise in protecting systems, managing threats, and ensuring data integrity. These credentials are often essential for entry-level and advanced roles alike:

- **CompTIA Security+** (*offered by CompTIA*): This is a foundational certification covering essential security skills, including threat management, cryptography, and network security. It is ideal for beginners entering the cybersecurity field.

- **Certified Ethical Hacker (CEH)** (*offered by EC-Council*): This certification focuses on ethical hacking techniques, vulnerability assessment, and penetration testing.

- **CISSP (Certified Information Systems Security Professional)** (*offered by* ISC²): This is a globally recognized certification for experienced security professionals. It covers eight domains of information security, including risk management and security architecture.

- **CCSP (Certified Cloud Security Professional)** (*offered by ISC²*): This certification concentrates on cloud-specific security design and operations. Ideal for those managing cloud environments securely.

- **SSCP (Systems Security Certified Practitioner)** (*offered by ISC²*): This entry-level to mid-level certification focuses on hands-on IT administration and access controls.

- **CISA (Certified Information Systems Auditor)** (*offered by ISACA*): This is a recognized certification for professionals focusing on auditing, control, and assurance of information systems.

- **CISM (Certified Information Security Manager)** (*offered by ISACA*): This certification is geared toward professionals managing enterprise information security teams or strategy.

- **OSCP (Offensive Security Certified Professional)** (*offered by Offensive Security*): This is an advanced hands-on certification in penetration testing and exploit development.

- **GSEC (GIAC Security Essentials Certification)** (*offered by* GIAC): This certification covers information security concepts, networking, cryptography, and incident response. It is suitable for those in operational or technical security roles.

Recommended certifications for System Architecture

For those aiming to design large-scale systems or lead enterprise architecture, the following certifications validate advanced design, planning, and implementation skills across cloud and enterprise environments:

- **AWS Certified Solutions Architect – Professional** (*offered by* Amazon Web Services): This certification is for experienced architects designing distributed systems on AWS.
- **Microsoft Certified: Azure Solutions Architect Expert** (*offered by* Microsoft): This certification covers architecture design and implementation in Microsoft Azure environments.
- **TOGAF 9 Certification** (*offered by* The Open Group): This is a widely respected certification for enterprise architects, focusing on large-scale IT system design frameworks.

Certifications can be a powerful tool for building credibility — especially for those entering the field or switching tracks. They help validate technical knowledge and show commitment to learning. But certifications alone are not a substitute for real-world experience.

To make certifications meaningful, it's essential to back them up with hands-on practice. Employers truly value the ability to explain how a tool works, troubleshoot issues, and walk through a real project. To sum up: first comes knowledge, second comes certification.

It's also worth exploring cross-certification, especially as roles become more blended. For example, a cloud engineer with a cybersecurity certification (like Security+) is often more valuable than one with cloud skills alone. Similarly, a data analyst who understands basic DevOps or scripting can stand out in today's fast-moving environments.

Certifications can open doors to different opportunities, but it is real skills that keep them open.

Conclusion

Learning is the foundation of any IT career, but having a direction is crucial. By choosing the right learning method and knowing the right time to pursue certification, one can save time, boost confidence, and set the stage for real growth. The most effective learners do more than just watch tutorials or collect credentials; they're building knowledge that endures and can be applied in real-world scenarios.

Certifications can strengthen a resume, but they work best when backed by hands-on understanding. You must focus first on gaining practical skills and then use certifications to validate them.

In the next chapter, we'll explore how to turn learning into action — with strategies for gaining hands-on experience, building a focused learning plan, and avoiding common missteps.

Frequently Asked Questions

1. What's the best way to start building IT skills?

Ans. It's best to start with small steps and maintain consistency. You should focus on foundational tools like Excel, basic troubleshooting, or beginner-level software. Rather than solely watching videos, use hands-on tutorials, structured courses, and repeat practice.

2. Do I need to follow a course, or can I self-learn everything?

Ans. Both works. If you're disciplined and good at navigating material, self-learning can work. If you need structure, support, or feedback, instructor-led courses are often more effective. Some people do both.

3. How do I choose the right learning platform?

Ans. You should choose the platform based on your budget, learning style, and goals. Free platforms (such as YouTube, Coursera, or Microsoft Learn) are great for beginners. Paid ones (such as Udemy, LinkedIn Learning, or bootcamps) offer depth, structure, and sometimes also provide certificates.

4. How much time should I spend learning each week?

Ans. One should aim for five to ten hours each week to start learning— enough to build momentum without burning out. The key is consistency, not cramming. Progress is built by regularly showing up, not by going all-in for a few days.

5. Do I need certifications to prove I've learned something?

Ans. Certifications can help, but aren't required. Employers often care more about what you can do than what certificate you hold. Build a project portfolio or be ready to explain what you've practiced.

6. What if I feel stuck or overwhelmed while learning?

Ans. That's normal. Take breaks, go back to earlier topics, ask questions in forums, or switch formats (for example, from videos to projects). Sometimes, all you need is a small win or a simpler explanation.

7. When should I start applying what I've learned?

Ans. It is best to do it right away. Apply every concept as soon as possible — even in small projects or personal tasks. Waiting to "master" everything before using it slows learning and kills motivation.

Quick Checklist

You can use this checklist to review your progress and track what you've done. Check off each item as you complete it.

☐ I've chosen a learning format that works for me (self-paced, instructor-led, and so on).

☐ I've explored free and paid platforms that offer training for my IT track.

☐ I've set a consistent weekly learning goal (for example, 5–10 hours).

☐ I've started learning with one core tool or concept.

☐ I apply what I learn through practice or projects (not just watching videos).

☐ I've created a simple learning plan (for 4–12 weeks).

☐ I understand that progress matters more than perfection.

☐ I've accepted that feeling stuck is normal, and I have strategies to move forward.

Tip: *You don't need to check every box right now. Use this list as a progress tracker, and revisit it as you move forward.*

CHAPTER 7
Turn Learning into Action

Introduction

This chapter focuses on turning theory into results. It covers how to create a realistic learning plan, what common mistakes to avoid, and how to start building experience — even before landing a job.

Whether starting or switching careers, the goal here is simple: take action that actually moves things forward.

This chapter will cover the following topics:
- Building a learning plan
- Pitfalls to avoid while learning
- How to gain experience without a job
- What if you fall off track?

Building a Learning Plan

Learning without a plan can become overwhelming. There are endless courses, tools, and opinions, but real progress comes from structure and consistency. A simple and focused learning plan can turn good intentions into real momentum.

This section provides a framework for building a plan based on available time, goals, and the career path selected. It's not about cramming everything at once — it's about building knowledge in manageable layers.

1. **Set a time commitment**: You need to start by being realistic about how much time can be consistently dedicated to learning each week. For most working professionals or students, 8–10 hours per week is a solid target, roughly 1 to 2 hours per day. If more time is available, great, but consistency matters more than intensity.

   Complex or technical topics, such as those in AI and Machine Learning, may require additional time to fully grasp — and that's okay. Adjust your schedule or extend certain weeks if needed to ensure understanding without rushing the process.

2. **Focus on 3 core areas**: A perfect balance of the following three areas prevents the trap of passive learning:

   - **Concepts**: Understand the "why" behind tools and practices
   - **Tools**: Get familiar with the actual software, platforms, and commands used in the job
   - **Practice**: Build something, test it, break it, and fix it

3. **Use a 12-week learning plan**: You can use this 12-week plan as a practical roadmap and personal tracker. Each week includes a focused activity, explanation, and real-world example to help you build momentum. Rather than thinking in months, this structure breaks your learning into clear and manageable steps, making it easier to stay consistent, build skills, and see real progress.

12-Week Learning Plan: Structure with Purpose

The following table outlines a 12-week learning plan designed to help build skills steadily and intentionally. Each week focuses on a specific task, with context and examples to guide application. Use it as a roadmap and tracker to stay consistent and turn learning into real progress.

Week	Learning Activity	Comment	Example
1	Set your learning track	Research your chosen tech. Understand the basics and what the role involves.	Choose Tableau. Watch beginner videos and read introductory blogs.
2	Study the fundamentals	Focus on core concepts. Download a trial version or free edition to get hands-on. Check for any prerequisites.	Download Tableau Public. Brush up on Excel or SQL if needed.
3	Learn step-by-step through practical application	Use self-learning or instructor-led formats, but stick to one path. Apply what you learn with hands-on practice.	Learn Tableau hands-on by self-learning or taking a structured instructor-led training.
4	Deepen concept understanding	Dive into advanced topics. Reinforce learning through exercises and challenges.	Practice advanced Tableau features like calculated fields and filters.
5	Engage with the user community	Join online forums and communities. Read posts, ask questions, and learn from others.	Join the Tableau Community. Browse solutions and ask or answer questions.
6	Build a project portfolio	Create a project using what you've learned. Take screenshots or save your work.	Design 2-3 Tableau dashboards and publish on Tableau Public.

Table 7.1: Weeks 1-6: Foundation and Practice

That marks the end of Week 6 Checkpoint. You've built a foundation, practiced hands-on, and connected with the community. Next, you need to showcase your skills and prepare for real-world opportunities, which we will discuss in the following table:

Week	Learning Activity	Comment	Example
7	Share your work publicly	Publish your work on public platforms and write short blogs or posts to showcase progress.	Write a blog post summarizing your project and what you learned.
8.	Explore related technologies	Look into technologies that complement your main skillset to broaden your perspective.	Explore Power BI to understand similarities and differences with Tableau.
9	Document your progress	Keep notes of completed lessons, projects, and skills. Identify next learning goals.	Create a progress doc with screenshots, Tableau Public links, or written summaries.
10	Update your resume	Start updating your resume with tools, projects, and accomplishments.	Add Tableau/Power BI skills and project highlights to your resume.
11	Practice articulating your knowledge	Prepare to explain what you've learned clearly, with or without a screen.	Practice describing your project as if in an interview, without demos.
12	Review and refine your plan	Reflect on your 12-week journey. Finish what's incomplete and plan your next steps.	Check what's complete. Refine your plan or set goals for the next 3 months.

Table 7.2: Weeks 7 – 12: Showcase and Prepare for the Job Market

Tip: Documenting what you learn helps reinforce memory, track your progress, and provides a quick reference when preparing for certifications or interviews. Your notes don't need to be perfect — bullet points, links, screenshots, or even scribbles work well. They become your personal repository of knowledge; you can access them anytime.

A structured plan turns learning from an abstract goal into something real and monitorable process. By committing to minor actions on weekly basis — and adapting as needed — progress becomes visible and motivating. Whether the focus is QA, cloud, data, or support, this kind of momentum helps build not just knowledge, but confidence.

Pitfalls to Avoid While Learning

It's easy to get excited about learning a new tool or choosing an IT career path, but without a clear approach, progress can quickly come to a halt. Many learners lose momentum because they jump in too fast, attempt too much, or focus on the incorrect things.

Here are some of the most common mistakes to avoid:

- **Jumping into a technology without understanding it**: Starting to learn a tool or platform without knowing what it's used for, or whether it aligns with your career goals, can lead to wasted effort. Take time to research the role, the real-world use of the technology, and the basic requirements before diving in.
- **Jumping between too many resources**: Switching between five different tutorials at once might feel productive, but it often results in shallow learning. Stick with one quality resource at a time and finish it before moving to the next.
- **Learning without doing**: Passive watching doesn't build any skill. Make sure you practice every concept

hands-on — whether it's writing test cases, setting up a cloud instance, or building a small dashboard.

- **Focusing only on certifications**: Certifications can boost your profile, but they don't replace real understanding. Use them as a supplement, not a shortcut.

- **Waiting for perfection**: You don't need to "know everything" before building your first project or applying for roles. Begin with small things. Learn by doing. Fail fast. Fix it.

- **Ignoring soft skills**: While having strong technical skills are important, but clear communication, proper documentation of your work, and collaboration are just as critical in real-world IT jobs.

- **Not asking for help**: Learning alone doesn't mean learning in isolation. Join online forums, follow LinkedIn voices, and ask questions. Getting stuck is normal — getting help moves you forward.

- **Skipping Reflection**: If you don't stop to review, you'll forget what you've learned. Check in every couple of weeks: What have you actually retained? What can you explain or apply?

Tip: Use a weekly journal or checklist to track what you've learned — and where you struggled. Progress feels real when you see it.

Avoiding these common pitfalls can save weeks — even months — of wasted effort. Staying consistent, asking questions, and taking action early makes the difference between passive learning and real growth.

How to Gain Experience Without a Job

One of the biggest challenges in starting an IT career is breaking the "no experience, no job" cycle. The good news? You don't need to wait for a company to give you a title before you start building real, valuable experience.

Here are smart, practical ways to get hands-on and prove your skills — even before your first role:

- **Build Personal Projects:** Nothing beats creating something from scratch. Whether it's a test plan, a small web app, a dashboard, or a cloud deployment — projects are proof of skill. Focus on real-world scenarios: a bug-tracking report, a mock website, or a mini data pipeline.

- **Contribute to Open Source:** Many open-source projects welcome contributors, especially for testing, documentation, and beginner-level features. Start by fixing bugs, improving documentation, or testing releases, and document what you did.

- **Join Hackathons or Online Challenges:** Participate in online coding or testing challenges (for example, Kaggle, HackerRank, Test Automation University, or community hackathons). These give you deadlines, teamwork, and practical scenarios — all resume-friendly.

- **Volunteer your SKILLS**: You should Offer to help a local nonprofit, school, or small business. You might build a basic website, troubleshoot IT issues, or design simple dashboards. These are real clients, and that's real experience.

- **Document your work**: Keep track of what you've built and learned. Utilize GitHub, Notion, LinkedIn, or even a Google Doc to showcase projects, notes, screenshots, and lessons.

- **Simulate a real workflow**: Don't just learn tools — use them as they're part of a job. Log test cases in a spreadsheet. Use Git for version control. Organize work in Trello or Jira. These habits show maturity.

- **Publish what you learn**: Write short posts or videos explaining your projects, the tools you tried, or problems you solved. This builds visibility and helps recruiters or hiring managers see your initiative.

Experience isn't just about having a job — it's about showing that you can solve problems, build things, and think like a professional. Projects, practice, and self-initiated work count. What matters most is being able to talk about what you've done and how you approached it.

What If You Fall Off Track?

Missing a few study sessions or falling behind on your plan doesn't mean you've failed; it means you're human. Life happens, motivation dips, and priorities shift. What matters most is not staying perfect — it's learning how to reset without giving up.

Here's how to refocus and move forward:

- **Pause and Reassess**: Take a short step back and ask:
    - What got in the way?
    - Was the plan too ambitious?
    - Am I still excited about the track I chose?

    A quick check-in helps uncover whether you need to adjust your approach, not abandon it.

- **Trim the plan, not the goal**: You don't have to quit — just simplify. Shorten your weekly goals. Pick one thing to focus on for the next 7 days. Success builds momentum.

- **Reconnect with Why You Started:** Write down (again) why this goal matters to you. Is it a new career? Better pay? Job security? A stronger sense of purpose?

- **Keep it visible**: a sticky note, a phone reminder, a journal entry.

- **Build a win streak**: Commit to 3–4 small tasks over the next week. Do them consistently. The goal is to rebuild belief and rhythm, not perfection.

- **Get Accountability**: Tell someone what you're working on — a peer, mentor, or even a LinkedIn post. Having others know what you're aiming for helps you stay on track.

- **Consider Instructor-Led or Structured Learning**: If self-paced learning isn't working, switch it up. A structured course with a live instructor or mentor can provide accountability, clearer timelines, and a more focused path. Sometimes, having someone guide you — and answer questions — is all it takes to regain momentum.

Tip: Falling off the plan isn't failure. Giving up on the goal is. Start again, start small, and keep moving.

Conclusion

Taking action is what separates intention from progress. Whether it's creating a learning plan, avoiding common traps, or building hands-on experience before landing a job — consistent, focused effort is what builds confidence and skill.

No one's path is perfect. What matters is showing up, learning from setbacks, and continuing to move forward.

In the next chapter, we'll look at how to turn those skills and experiences into a strong job application, with clear guidance on resumes, portfolios, and interview prep.

Frequently Asked Questions

1. How do I start applying what I've learned if I don't have a job yet?

Ans. You can start by building projects, recreating real-world tasks, and documenting your work. Publish your projects online or share them with peers. Action builds confidence and shows initiative to future employers.

2. What if I don't feel ready to take action yet?

Ans. You may never feel 100% ready — action builds readiness. Start with a simple step, even if it's revisiting what you've learned and turning it into a checklist, blog post, or small project.

3. How do I build a 12-week learning plan that works?

Ans. Break down your goal into weekly checkpoints. Include time for learning, practicing, reviewing, and sharing. Keep it realistic — even 1 hour a day adds up fast.

4. Do I need to finish learning everything before applying for jobs?

Ans. No. Start applying once you've built a foundation and can show basic skills or projects. Many employers value learners who take initiative and demonstrate potential.

5. How do I get experience without having a job?

Ans. You can contribute to open source, help friends or nonprofits, replicate public datasets, or do mock projects. The goal is to build and show real work, even if it's self-directed.

6. What if I can't follow my plan consistently?

Ans. That's normal. Adjust the pace, simplify tasks, or shift focus — but don't stop. Progress isn't about perfection; it's about steady movement forward.

Quick Checklist

You can use this checklist to review your progress and track what you've done. Check off each item as you complete it.

☐ I've taken a small first step toward applying what I've learned.

☐ I've chosen one project idea or task to work on (real or mock).

☐ I'm documenting my work and progress along the way.

☐ I understand the value of creating a 12-week learning and action plan.

☐ I've explored online communities, forums, or user groups in my track.

☐ I've considered publishing or sharing a project publicly.

☐ I understand that action creates clarity, not the other way around.

☐ I've reflected on what to refine or do next in my learning process.

Tip: You don't need to check every box right now. Use this list as a progress tracker, and revisit it as you move forward.

CHAPTER 8
Preparing for the Job Market

Introduction

Once the skills are in place, the next challenge is getting noticed and getting hired. This chapter focuses on how to present experience, build a strong resume, use LinkedIn effectively, and prepare for interviews with confidence. The goal is to bridge the final gap between learning and landing the first role.

This chapter will cover the following topics:

- Building a Job-Ready resume
- Using LinkedIn to get noticed
- Preparing for Interviews
- Finding IT job opportunities
- Navigating the job hunt

Building a Job-Ready Resume

A resume is more than a list of skills — it's your first impression. For entry-level IT roles, it tells hiring managers what you know, what you're working toward, and how you can contribute.

The objective of a resume is to:

- Show that you're ready to contribute and eager to grow
- Highlight your relevant skills, tools, and certifications
- Give a snapshot of your projects and learning progress
- Help hiring managers see your potential quickly

What makes a Strong resume?

Hiring managers aren't just looking for a perfect list of skills — they want to see potential, focus, and the ability to apply knowledge in real ways. A well-crafted resume should quickly answer the question: Can this person contribute in a meaningful way?

Here's what tends to stand out:

- **Practical skills:** List tools and technologies you've worked with — even during training or personal projects (for example, SQL, Python, Java, Excel).

- **Relevant projects:** Demonstrate how you've applied skills in real or simulated environments. A portfolio project or hands-on lab work matters more than generic course completion.

- **Clarity and readability:** The resume should have a clean formatting, consistent structure, and should be easy to skim in under 10 seconds.

- **Progress and initiative:** Self-study, certifications, and community involvement (for example, GitHub, blogs, open-source work) show motivation and follow-through.

Crafting a Resume

Now that we know what hiring managers are looking for, the next step is putting those elements together in a clear and professional format. A strong resume doesn't need to be long — it needs to be focused, relevant, and easy to read.

Things to include in a resume are as follows:

- **Summary or Objective:** Provide a short introduction (2-3 lines) stating your objectives and the value you offer
- **Skills/Tools:** Grouped into categories (such as "Languages," "Databases," "Soft Skills")
- **Education or Background:** Formal or informal — include if it's relevant
- **Certifications/Training:** List any structured learning
- **Projects:** Include one or two short examples, even if personal or course-based

Sample Resume

The following example shows how a beginner or career switcher can build a strong resume, even without formal IT job experience. It highlights certifications, tools, and personal projects in a clear, professional layout.

Use this as an inspiration to structure your resume, focusing on what's relevant and practical for your target role.

[Your Name]
[City, State] · [Phone Number] · [Email] · [LinkedIn URL] · [Portfolio Link]

Professional Summary

Motivated and detail-oriented IT professional with hands-on experience in data analysis, technical support, and troubleshooting through training and personal projects. Strong foundation in Excel, SQL, and system administration. Actively pursuing a career in [insert focus area: support, data, QA, etc.].

Technical Skills

- **Tools and Platforms:** Excel, PowerPoint, Microsoft 365, Windows 10
- **Languages:** SQL, Python
- **Databases:** Oracle, MySQL
- **Other:** GitHub, Tableau Public, Jira, ServiceNow

Certifications

- IT Support Professional Certificate
- Microsoft Certified: Azure Fundamentals
- Tableau Data Analytics Badge

Education / Training

- Instructor-led training in Data Analytics – [Training Provider Name]
- Self-paced SQL Bootcamp
- Bachelor's in Business Administration – [University Name]

Projects

IT Support Troubleshooting Lab (Self-paced Training)

- Diagnosed simulated issues related to system access, software installation, and connectivity
- Created support documentation and escalation notes

Sales Dashboard (Tableau Public)
- Developed an interactive dashboard using an open dataset
- Filtered data by region, created visual KPIs, and presented insights

SQL Query Practice
- Wrote SQL queries to filter, join, and summarize e-commerce data
- Built reusable scripts and tracked progress using GitHub

Additional Highlights
- Member of the [Local] Tech Networking Group
- Attended virtual webinars on IT career pathways and cloud trends
- Volunteer: Tech setup and troubleshooting for local non-profit events

A resume doesn't need to be packed with job titles to be effective. What matters most is clarity, relevance, and proof of progress. By highlighting skills, certifications, and hands-on projects, even a newcomer can stand out. Focus on what's been learned, what's been built, and where the journey is headed — that's what gets noticed.

Using LinkedIn to Get Noticed

LinkedIn isn't just a digital resume— it's a visibility tool. When used well, it helps recruiters and hiring managers discover your skills, see your progress, and get a sense of who you are as a professional.

Even if you're just starting, a polished LinkedIn profile can make a big difference.

Let's see what to include on your profile page:

- **Professional Photo**: Use a clear, friendly headshot — no filters or casual settings.
- **Headline**: Mention your focus area (for example, "Aspiring IT Support Specialist" or "Data Analyst in Training").
- **About Section**: Write 2–3 short paragraphs explaining what you're learning, what you're building, and what you're aiming to do next.
- **Experience Section**: Add any relevant training, personal projects, volunteer work, or freelance tasks.
- **Skills Section**: List tools and technologies you've learned (for example, SQL, Tableau, Python, Azure, Excel).
- **Certifications**: Add any completed training or industry-recognized certificates — these build credibility.
- **Projects**: Link to GitHub, Tableau Public, blogs, or anything that shows your work in action.

The following are some of the best practices for visibility of your LinkedIn page:

- **Post updates**: Share milestones, projects, or certifications — even a short post can help build your presence.

  Engage with others: Commenting on relevant content, following companies, or joining tech communities helps you stay visible.

- **Connect with intentions**: Reach out to classmates, instructors, mentors, or professionals in your desired field. A short, polite message goes a long way.

  Tip: Use keywords from job descriptions in your profile, especially in your headline and skills section. Recruiters search by keyword.

Sample Beginner LinkedIn "About" Section

Aspiring IT professional with a background in customer service and a growing skill set in technical support, data analysis, and system troubleshooting.

Currently completing certifications in IT support and cloud fundamentals, and building hands-on experience with tools like Excel, SQL, and Tableau.

I'm passionate about solving problems, learning new technologies, and contributing to teams that value growth, reliability, and continuous improvement. Open to entry-level IT roles, internships, and support positions.

You don't need years of experience to create a strong LinkedIn presence — just clarity, consistency, and effort. When your profile reflects what you're learning and where you're headed, it becomes more than a resume. It becomes a signal that you're active, intentional, and ready for opportunity.

Preparing for Interviews

Interviews are the moment when all learning, preparation, and development are assessed— but they don't have to be intimidating. With the right preparation, even a beginner can walk in with confidence and leave a strong impression.

Whether it's for a help desk role, a QA position, or a junior data analyst job, most entry-level IT interviews will focus on two things:

1) Can you communicate clearly?

2) Do you have a grasp of the tools or concepts you say you know?

What to Expect in IT Interviews

Most interviews follow a mix of formats: some questions test soft skills while others check your technical understanding. Here's what typically shows up in an IT interview:

- **Behavioral Questions**: These questions test how you think and communicate — not just your knowledge: *Tell me about a time you solved a problem. How do you handle deadlines or technical issues?*
- **Technical Basics**: You may be asked to explain a concept, describe a tool you've used, or solve a simple problem. Example:
  - *What does a JOIN do in SQL?*
  - *What steps would you take if a user can't access a shared folder?*
- **Scenario Questions**: Expect *"what would you do if..."* questions. These help assess your problem-solving skills and logic, not necessarily your final answer.

The Most Important Question in Any Interview

It almost always starts the same way: **"Tell me about yourself."**

It sounds simple, but this is one of the most important — and most overlooked — questions in any interview. It's your first chance to set the tone, highlight your strengths, and guide the conversation toward what you want them to notice.

Let's discuss what the interviewers want to hear:

- A summary of who you are professionally (not personally)
- A quick mention of your current focus (what you're learning or doing)
- A hint of where you're headed or what you're looking for

Example (Beginner/Transitioning into IT):

Here's an example of how to answer the "Tell me about yourself" question if you're coming from a non-technical background and transitioning into a Business Intelligence role:

I come from a customer support background and recently transitioned into IT after completing structured training in data analysis and business intelligence. I've worked on hands-on projects using Excel, SQL, and Tableau to create reports and dashboards from real-world datasets. Right now, I'm looking for a role where I can continue developing my BI skills, contribute to data-driven decision-making, and grow into a long-term career in analytics.

Mastering the Interview Process

A strong interview isn't just about what you know — it's about how well you explain it. Whether the questions are technical or behavioral, preparation is what builds confidence and helps you stand out.

This section covers what to review, how to practice, and how to get ready for different interview formats — whether online, on the phone, or face-to-face.

Know your resume

- **Review your projects and portfolio**: Be ready to explain what you built, why you built it, and what you learned from it.
- **Anticipate follow-up questions**: If your resume says "SQL project," know which functions you used, what challenges you faced, and how you solved them.

Revisit core skills and tools:

- Brush up on tools mentioned in the job description — Excel, Tableau, SQL, and so on.
- Review common questions for your track (for example, "What does a JOIN do in SQL?" or "How do you approach testing a login page?")
- Make flashcards or a cheat sheet to quickly refresh key terms or processes.

Practice talking out loud:

- Record yourself answering basic questions like "Tell me about yourself" or "What's your biggest strength?"
- Practice explaining your projects and tools as if you're teaching someone else.
- If you struggle to describe your work simply, keep refining until it feels natural.

Interview Formats and Preparation Tips

Not all interviews happen in the same way. Be ready for these three common formats:

- **Phone Interviews**: These are often short, first-round screenings. Speak clearly, avoid filler words, and keep notes nearby — but don't read from a script. Find a quiet place with a good signal.
- **Video Interviews**: Dress professionally and set up in a clean, quiet space. Test your camera, mic, and internet ahead of time. Look into the camera while speaking, and avoid distracting tabs or notifications.

- **In-Person Interviews**: Bring printed copies of your resume, arrive early, and be ready for a mix of technical and behavioral questions. Use positive body language, make eye contact, and be polite to everyone — not just the interviewer.

> *Tip*: Do a mock interview in each format with a friend or mentor. It helps uncover habits or technical issues before they become problems.

End-of-Interview Questions

Don't leave the interview without asking a few thoughtful questions. It shows curiosity, preparation, and genuine interest in the role and the team.

- "What does a typical day look like in this role?"
- "What kind of onboarding or training do new hires receive?"
- "What tools does the team use most often?"

Success in interviews isn't just about memorizing answers — it's about knowing your story, practicing with purpose, and showing up prepared and confident. The more you prepare, the more each interview becomes an opportunity instead of an obstacle.

Finding IT Job Opportunities

Once your resume is polished and your LinkedIn is live, the next step is knowing where to actually look for roles. IT jobs are posted across a variety of platforms — but not all are created equal, and some are better suited for entry-level roles or career switchers.

The following are the most common and effective places to start your search:

- **Job Boards**: These are the most widely used platforms for job hunting:
  - **LinkedIn Jobs**: They are ideal for networking and applying. Many listings show if you're a good match based on your profile.
  - **Indeed**: It has a broad reach; great for both entry-level and contract roles.
  - **Dice**: It focuses on tech jobs only. It had helpful filters for skills and experience levels.
  - **Glassdoor**: It lets you research salaries and company reviews while browsing listings.
  - **HackerRank/Codingame**: Some companies recruit directly through coding challenge platforms.

  Tip: Use filters to narrow down to "entry-level," "internship," or "junior" roles and set alerts so you don't miss any new listings.

- **Company Career Pages**: If you have a few companies in mind (like Nationwide, Infosys, IBM, or Salesforce), go directly to their careers page. Large organizations often post jobs here before sharing them on other platforms.

- **Staffing Agencies and Tech Recruiters**: Many IT professionals secure their first job through staffing agencies. Look for those that specialize in technology (such as TEKsystems, Robert Half Technology, Modis).

- **Local or Online Communities**: A Few examples are as follows:
  - Join Slack groups, Discord servers, or LinkedIn communities focused on tech careers.
  - Follow hashtags like #Hiring or #TechJobs on LinkedIn and Twitter/X.
  - Platforms like Reddit (for example, r/ITCareerQuestions) often share job leads and advice.
- **Alumni Networks and Referrals**: Reach out to people from your training program, college, or professional network. Many roles get filled through referrals before ever being posted online.

Navigating the Job Hunt

Getting your first IT job isn't just about applying everywhere and hoping for the best. Strategy is important — from interpreting job descriptions the right way to handling rejection and staying motivated. This section breaks down how to approach the job search with a strategy, rather than relying on chance.

Reading a Job Description

IT job descriptions can be intimidating, especially with long lists of skills and tools. But not everything listed is a hard requirement.

Let's see what to look for in the job description:

- **Core skills**: It includes the skills mentioned more than once — these are usually non-negotiable (for example, SQL, Cloud, Python).

- **Job title versus responsibilities**: Sometimes, the position of "Systems Analyst" actually functions as a support role. Focus on responsibilities, rather than the title.

- **Level indicators**: Look for terms like "junior," "entry-level," or "0–2 years of experience."

  Tip: *If you meet 60–70% of the requirements and can demonstrate learning ability, you're qualified enough to apply.*

Applying for a Job Strategically

Not every job needs a different resume, but every job deserves a tailored application.

Here are the steps to apply smarter:

1. Customize your summary or headline to match the job's focus.
2. Use keywords from the job description — especially skills, tools, or certifications.
3. Add a brief, targeted message when applying through LinkedIn or via email.
4. Track where you've applied to avoid double submissions and follow up professionally.

Dealing with Rejections

It's normal to get ignored or rejected — particularly in the beginning. What matters is how you respond. Let's look at some pointers:

- **Don't take silence personally**: Many recruiters only respond when a candidate is selected to move forward in the process.

- **Review and Improve**: After an interview, reflect on what went well and what could be improved. Write down any questions you remember — they'll help you prepare better for the next one.
- **Keep learning**: Between job applications, work on your portfolio, sharpen your interview answers, or complete relevant certifications.
- **Celebrate small wins**: Getting a call back, improving your answers, or finishing a mock interview.

Job searching isn't just about sending out resumes — it's about reading between the lines, staying focused, and acquiring knowledge along the way. A thoughtful, steady approach will always beat a rushed one.

Conclusion

Getting hired in IT takes more than just technical know-how — it takes strategy, preparation, and self-awareness. From crafting a strong resume to making the most of LinkedIn, interviews, and job searches, every piece helps build your professional presence. The more prepared you are, the more confident you'll feel when opportunity shows up.

In the next chapter, the focus shifts to long-term growth — staying relevant, leveling up, and building a sustainable, future-ready career in IT.

Frequently Asked Questions

1. When should I start preparing my resume?

Ans. As soon as you've completed a project or learned a relevant skill, start building your resume. You don't need to wait until everything is perfect — update it as you grow.

2. What should I highlight on a beginner-level IT resume?

Ans. You must focus on transferable skills, learning achievements, and small projects. Show what you can do, not just what you've studied. Employers look for initiative and the ability to solve problems.

3. Do I need a LinkedIn profile even if I'm not active on social media?

Ans. Yes. LinkedIn is a digital resume and networking tool, not social media in the traditional sense. Recruiters often find candidates through LinkedIn, even if they aren't actively posting.

4. How do I explain a career switch or gap in my resume?

Ans. Be honest and focus on what you've learned or done during that time. Use your summary or cover letter to frame your story. Emphasize your motivation, skills, and readiness to work.

5. How do I prepare for interviews with little experience?

Ans. Practice explaining your projects, what tools you used, what you learned, and how you solved problems. Focus on communication, curiosity, and a learning mindset — these go a long way.

6. What if I keep applying and don't hear back?

Ans. Don't take it personally. Job hunting takes time. Get feedback on your resume, improve your LinkedIn, apply in smaller batches, and focus on quality over quantity. Every rejection is a redirection.

Quick Checklist

You can use this checklist to review your progress and track what you've done. Check off each item as you complete it.

☐ I've started building or updating my resume with relevant skills and projects.

☐ I've set up or refreshed my LinkedIn profile.

☐ I've reviewed and practiced describing my projects or learning experiences clearly.

☐ I understand what to expect in IT job interviews.

☐ I've begun applying for roles that match my skill level and interests.

☐ I've researched companies or industries I want to work in.

☐ I've prepared for behavioral and technical interview questions.

☐ I've created a simple job tracking system (for example, a spreadsheet or a notebook).

Tip: You don't need to check every box right now. Use this list as a progress tracker, and revisit it as you move forward.

CHAPTER 9
Advancing a Career in IT

Introduction

Getting your first job in tech is a major milestone — but it's just the beginning. The real challenge (and opportunity) is building a career that grows with the industry, adapts to change, and aligns with long-term goals.

This chapter explores what it takes to keep progressing — from staying current with skills to finding mentorship, setting direction, and making strategic moves as the technological landscape evolves.

This chapter will cover the following topics:

- Staying relevant
- Advancing in the current role
- Pursuing specialization
- Setting and tracking career goals

Staying Relevant

Technology changes fast, and so does the job market. New tools emerge, skills go out of date, and employers expect professionals who can adapt. Staying relevant in IT doesn't mean learning every trend. It means staying sharp, building on what's already known, and knowing when to pivot.

Here are a few practical ways to stay relevant:

1. **Set a learning rhythm**: Block out regular time each week to learn — even if it's just one hour. This could be for reading documentation, watching short tutorials, or reviewing changelogs for tools you use.

2. **Learn new technology**: Instead of piecing together scattered tutorials, take a structured, instructor-led course. A well-designed class can help you learn more in less time, with clear direction, hands-on practice, and answers to questions when you need them.

3. **Follow trusted sources**: Instead of trying to keep up with everything, choose a few curated, high-quality sources, such as:

   - Official blogs from Microsoft, AWS, or Google
   - LinkedIn posts from thought leaders in your track
   - Trusted technological blogs or newsletters

4. **Build with new tools**: The best way to learn a new tool is to use it — even in small ways. Try replicating an old project in a newer platform or experimenting with a tool your team hasn't explored yet.

5. **Join tech communities**: Engaging with online groups helps you stay updated on trends, tools, and real-world discussions happening in your field.

6. **Learn adjacent skills**: If you're in support, learn basic scripting. If you're in data, explore dashboards or cloud basics. Expanding just outside your core role keeps your profile dynamic and your skill set more valuable.

7. **Keep portfolio and profiles updated**: As you learn, build, and grow, make sure your online presence reflects that. Update LinkedIn, your resume, or your GitHub with the latest tools, projects, and achievements.

Staying relevant isn't about chasing every trend — it's about being curious, intentional, and committed to continued growth.

Advancing in the Current Role

Career growth doesn't always require changing jobs. In many cases, meaningful progress happens by deepening skills, taking initiative, and increasing visibility — right where you are. The key is to treat every role as a platform for growth, not just a task list to complete.

Here are some ways to advance without switching companies (or even teams):

- **Master the Fundamentals**: Get good at the core responsibilities of the role. Reliability builds trust, and trust opens doors. Whether it's troubleshooting, documentation, reporting, or automation, consistency earns visibility.

- **Take Ownership**: Look for small problems that haven't been solved yet, and offer to take the lead. These don't have to be complex — even optimizing a manual process or improving a checklist shows initiative.

- **Understand the Bigger Picture**: Spend time understanding how your work connects to the bigger picture. Learn about related tools, processes, or teams. For example, a QA tester could explore how releases are managed, or a support analyst might learn the basics of scripting to automate routine tasks.

- **Seek and Apply Feedback**: Regular feedback — from peers or supervisors — is one of the most useful tools for growth. Ask what you're doing well and where you can improve. Then, act on it and follow up to show progress.

- **Upskill Strategically**: Take training in areas that support your team's work or prepare you for the next level. If you're in support, learn scripting. If you're in analytics, dive into data visualization.

- **Document and Share**: Keep track of what you've improved, created, or contributed to and share it appropriately (in meetings, performance reviews, or team chats). It's not about bragging — it's about showing growth and value.

- **Keep the Resume Updated**: Even small wins — like completing a project, learning a new tool, or improving a process — deserve a place on your resume. Don't wait until you're job-hunting. Keep it current so you're always ready for internal moves, promotions, or unexpected opportunities. Consider your resume as a live document that reflects your growth beyond just job titles.

Advancement doesn't always mean changing jobs — it often starts by doing more with the role already in hand. Taking initiative, learning beyond the basics, and documenting progress can turn a current position into a launchpad for long-term growth.

Pursuing Specialization

In the early stages of an IT career, it's common to try different areas such as support, QA, cloud, or analytics. But over time, specializing in a specific domain can open new doors, lead to higher pay, and make it easier to stand out in a competitive field.

The following points can help guide that decision:

- **No rush**: It's okay to stay general early on. Exposure to multiple domains helps build context and confidence. Specialization tends to be more valuable once core skills are solid and interests are clearer.

- **Follow market demand**: Look for the intersection between your skills, your passions, and market demands. For example, if data analysis clicks for you and there's rising demand in your industry, that's a good signal.

- **Test focus areas**: Before committing to a specialty, try building a personal project or taking on a related task at work.

- **Seek mentorship**: Talk to someone who is already on that path. Ask about the actual responsibilities of the role, the most important skills, and the challenges they encounter. Firsthand input helps to avoid unrealistic expectations.

- **Targeted learning**: Once a focus area is chosen, delve into it thoroughly. Participate in structured and role-specific training. Get certified if it helps to prove your skill level. And make sure to build real examples.

- **Evolve**: Specializing doesn't lock you in. Roles, tools, and interests change, and many IT professionals shift paths or broaden their focus as they grow.

Specialization isn't about narrowing options — it's about building depth where it matters most. With the right timing and focus, it becomes a powerful step toward long-term career growth.

Setting and Tracking Career Goals

Advancing in IT is the result of consistent learning, deliberate choices, and a clear idea of what success looks like. Without defined goals, it's easy to stay busy but make little progress.

Setting clear, measurable goals create focus, and tracking them helps maintain momentum:

1. **Define progress**: Career growth looks different for everyone. For some, it's about becoming a senior engineer. For others, it's moving into leadership, switching tracks, or deepening a specialty. Start by identifying what growth *actually* means for your career.

2. **Set goals**: Break down goals into timeframes as follows:
   - Short-term (3–6 months): Complete a certification, build a project, and contribute to a new area at work
   - Mid-term (6–18 months): Shift into a new specialty and grow your portfolio
   - Long-term (2+ years): Become a subject matter expert, transition into architecture or strategy, and lead a team

3. **Tracking method**: Track progress using a spreadsheet, planner, or app. Include what you're working on, what's completed, and what you want to improve. Even quick weekly notes help spot patterns and keep momentum going.

4. **Celebrate small wins**: Completing a project, learning a tool, or presenting in a team meeting are all markers of growth. Acknowledging these keeps your energy high for the long game.

5. **Regular reviews**: Conduct a review of your actual position compared to your planned position once a month or quarterly. As life changes, being flexible is important — but regular check-ins keep the path intentional rather than accidental.

Setting goals gives your career direction — tracking them turns that direction into momentum. Even small, steady progress adds up over time. Clarity, consistency, and course correction are the keys to long-term growth in technology.

Conclusion

Advancing your career in IT is about more than technical skill. It's about mindset, adaptability, and staying plugged into how the industry evolves. Whether you're pursuing certifications, shifting into a leadership role, or exploring new technologies, your career will keep growing as long as you keep learning.

This chapter outlined key strategies for advancing: staying current with evolving tech, deepening expertise through specialization, setting intentional career goals, and continuing to add value in your current role.

In the next chapter, we'll dive into developing AI literacy, using tools like ChatGPT and GitHub Copilot, and how to start working with AI — even as a beginner.

Frequently Asked Questions

1. How do I grow in my IT role after landing a job?

Ans. Keep learning on the job, take on stretch projects, ask questions, and document your progress. Small wins and consistency build long-term growth.

2. When should I start thinking about career advancement?

Ans. As soon as you feel comfortable in your current role. Set goals, look for gaps in your knowledge, and identify where you want to go next.

3. What's the difference between specializing and staying broad?

Ans. Specializing means going deep in a specific area, such as security, data, or cloud. Staying broad gives flexibility across roles. Many successful IT pros start broad and then specialize as their interests and opportunities grow.

4. Do I need to keep getting new certifications to stay relevant?

Ans. Not always. Certifications help, but hands-on experience, new projects, and understanding trends often matter more. Learn what's useful, not just what's popular.

5. How can I stay updated in a fast-changing industry?

Ans. Follow trusted blogs, attend webinars, take short courses, and join professional communities. Set aside regular time to explore and keep your skills sharp.

6. What if I feel stuck in my current role?

Ans. Talk to your manager, take on a new type of task, explore internal transfers, or start preparing for your next role outside the company. Feeling stuck is often a sign that it's time to stretch or shift.

Quick Checklist

You can use this checklist to review your progress and track what you've done. Check off each item as you complete it.

- ☐ I've set clear goals for my next phase of IT career growth.
- ☐ I've identified areas where I want to specialize or go deeper.
- ☐ I've looked for stretch projects or new responsibilities at work.
- ☐ I've updated my learning plan to include advanced tools or topics.

☐ I've found ways to mentor, teach, or share knowledge with others.

☐ I've joined a professional community or network in my field.

☐ I regularly review trends to stay current in my area of focus.

☐ I know that growth includes both skill-building and career planning.

Tip: You don't need to check every box right now. Use this list as a progress tracker, and revisit it as you move forward.

CHAPTER 10
AI Literacy for Tech Careers

Introduction

Artificial Intelligence (AI) is no longer just for researchers or advanced programmers. It has already become a part of modern IT work, whether you realize it or not. From writing code to troubleshooting systems and analyzing data, AI is transforming how tasks are accomplished. As someone entering or advancing in technology, you don't need to build AI tools, but you do need to grasp how to use them.

This chapter will help you build AI literacy — a foundational skill that will help you learn faster, work smarter, and stay relevant in an evolving industry.

This chapter will cover the following topics:

- Introducing AI literacy
- Prompting basics
- AI as a learning companion

Introducing AI Literacy

Artificial Intelligence (AI) refers to machines and software that can simulate human-like thinking, such as learning, reasoning, and problem-solving. It includes things like natural language processing, image recognition, predictive analytics, and automation. In the past, AI was something only data scientists or advanced developers worked with. Today, AI is showing up in everyday tools that professionals across IT roles use.

AI literacy means understanding how these tools work, how to interact with them effectively, and where they fit into your workflow. It's not about building algorithms — it's about being comfortable using AI to support learning, work, and decision-making.

Practical Uses of AI

AI doesn't replace learning — it supports it. For tech learners and early-career professionals, it can act like a second brain: simplifying concepts, speeding up tasks, and offering instant feedback.

Here are just a few practical ways it can assist:

- Summarize documentation or complex articles
- Explain technical terms in plain language
- Review code or scripts and suggest improvements
- Generate sample resumes, learning plans, or troubleshooting guides
- Create test cases, blog post ideas, or IT interview prep questions

Top AI Tools for Learning and Productivity

Many AI tools are now integrated into platforms used across IT, offering support for writing, coding, research, summarizing, and even automation. They're accessible to beginners and can dramatically improve productivity and learning when used well. Some of the popular tools include:

- **ChatGPT:** A conversational AI tool that can explain technical topics in simple terms, answer questions, draft summaries, review resumes, generate prompts, and even help troubleshoot code or workflows.

- **GitHub Copilot**: It is a coding assistant that works inside editors like Visual Studio Code. It suggests code completions, functions, and even entire blocks based on comments or existing code, especially useful for new developers learning by doing.

- **Gemini (by Google)**: This helps with research, summarizing long documents or webpages, answering questions based on multiple sources, and even generating ideas or content outlines.

- **Microsoft Copilot (Office 365)**: Built into apps like Word, Excel, and Outlook, it helps to generate content, summarize documents, write emails, analyze spreadsheets, and automate repetitive office tasks — making it a great tool for IT support, analysts, and project managers.

- **Replit Ghostwriter**: This is an AI coding assistant integrated into Replit's online IDE. It is excellent for beginners who are learning to code interactively in the browser.

Today, there are countless AI tools available, and most of them provide free versions or trials. Begin with the free tier — it's more than enough to learn the basics, experiment, and discover how these tools can support your work.

Being AI literate means knowing how to:

- Ask good questions (prompts) to get the best results
- Verify and apply what the AI suggests
- Utilize AI to complement your skills, rather than replace them.

Getting started with the AI Tool

The use of AI doesn't require any special software or hardware — many of the most widely used tools are free, web-based, and accessible to anyone with an internet connection. Here are some beginner-friendly AI platforms to try:

- **ChatGPT** (https://chat.openai.com/): Using ChatGPT, you can create a free account to ask questions, generate content, or explore IT concepts in a conversational format.
- **Perplexity AI** (https://www.perplexity.ai/): This tool focuses on fact-based responses with source citations — great for research and quick technical learning.
- **Gemini** (formerly **Bard**) (https://gemini.google.com/): This is Google's AI assistant, which is useful for summaries, document insights, and quick explanations.
- **GitHub Copilot** (https://github.com/features/copilot): This AI tool requires a GitHub account. It helps with code suggestions inside VS Code and is perfect for learners writing or reviewing scripts.
- **Notion AI** (https://www.notion.so/product/ai): This tool helps in generating notes, summaries, or blog drafts. It is also good for organizing learning projects.

Begin with whichever tool feels easiest. AI literacy is a career skill now. It's not optional anymore— it's a way to boost your efficiency, accelerate your learning, and stay relevant as technology evolves.

Prompting Basics

Prompting is the art of asking AI the right question in the right way. It's not about using perfect language — it's about being clear, specific, and intentional. A well-crafted prompt informs the AI what you want, how you want it, and what your context is. Consider it similar to providing a smart assistant with directions.

Basic Prompt formula

A good prompt gives the AI enough context to understand what's needed — and how to deliver it. Think of it as a short instruction that combines the task, your background, and the desired output format.

Use this simple formula to shape better prompts:

- **Task**: What do you want? (Explain, list, compare, summarize)
- **Context**: Who is it for? (Beginner, intermediate, job seeker)
- **Format**: How do you want the response? (Bullet points, paragraph, checklist)

Examples by use case

The best way to improve at prompting is to practice across real situations. The following are sample prompts tailored to common IT learning and job tasks:

- **Learning**: 'Explain the difference between RAM and ROM for beginners, using a table format.'
- **Resume help**: 'Rewrite this line to sound more professional: Helped users fix computer issues.'
- **Debugging**: 'What does this error mean in Python? [paste code snippet]'
- **Interview preparation**: 'Ask me 5 beginner-level questions about IT support with sample answers.'

Common Pitfalls to Avoid

Like any tool, AI works best when used thoughtfully. While experimenting is encouraged, there are some common pitfalls beginners should avoid to get accurate and safe results:

- Vague prompts like 'What is cloud computing?' (add context)
- Relying on AI without reviewing or understanding
- Sharing passwords, personal info, or sensitive data

AI as a Learning Companion

AI tools can be powerful learning companions — helping accelerate skill-building, close knowledge gaps, and support consistent progress.

Here's how AI can actively assist in learning:

1. **Explaining Concepts in Plain Language**: Struggling with a technical concept? Tools like ChatGPT can break it down in simple terms, provide analogies, or even walk through examples step-by-step. It's like having a patient tutor on standby.

   Example:
   "Explain how DNS works like I'm new to networking."
   "Summarize the difference between REST and GraphQL."

2. **Generating Practice Tasks**: AI can create coding exercises, quiz questions, or step-by-step challenges tailored to what you're trying to learn.

   Example:

   "Give me five beginner SQL challenges involving JOINs and GROUP BY."

   "Create a troubleshooting scenario for a help desk role."

3. **Reinforcing Retention**: AI can quiz or help you recall information over time. This reinforces learning through repetition and active recall — key to retaining new knowledge.

   Example:
   "Ask me 10 random questions on cloud fundamentals."

4. **Clarifying Errors or Debugging**: Stuck on a bug or an error message? Paste it into an AI tool to get help with interpreting the problem and understanding what to try next.

   Example:
   "Here's my Python code — why am I getting a TypeError on line 8?"

5. **Summarizing Content or Lessons:** AI can summarize videos, articles, or textbook chapters to give you a quick overview — especially helpful when reviewing or revising.

AI helps personalize learning, reduce friction, and encourage exploration. The more comfortable you get with asking the right questions or prompts, the more value you'll extract — not just as a user, but as an active learner shaping your own growth.

Conclusion

AI is already transforming how IT professionals learn, work, and solve problems. You don't need advanced technical skills to be AI-literate; it involves knowing how to use the right tools with clarity, purpose, and curiosity. Whether writing a resume, debugging code, or exploring a new concept, AI can act as a learning partner that grows with you.

Begin with small things. Build the habit. Utilize AI to sharpen your thinking — not to avoid it. That's how real skill develops.

Frequently Asked Questions

1. Do I need coding skills to start using AI tools?

Ans. No. Many AI tools are designed for non-programmers and are easy to use with natural language prompts.

2. Is it safe to use AI to learn technical topics?

Ans. Yes, but always cross-check the information. AI is helpful, but it can sometimes provide inaccurate or outdated responses.

3. Which AI tool is best for IT beginners?

Ans. Start with ChatGPT or Perplexity; they are accessible, free, and offer flexible support for learning, writing, and researching.

4. Can AI really help in preparing for interviews or certifications?

Ans. Absolutely. Use it to practice interview questions, explain complex topics, or summarize study notes.

Quick Checklist

You can use this checklist to review your understanding and actions. Check off each step as you complete it:

- ☐ Explored at least one AI tool (ChatGPT, Gemini, Perplexity)
- ☐ Practiced writing prompts for learning or research
- ☐ Used AI to explain a technical concept in simple terms
- ☐ Asked AI to help prepare for an interview or quiz
- ☐ Reviewed the limitations and safe use of AI tools
- ☐ Created or saved a few prompts you found helpful

Final Thoughts

A career in IT isn't built overnight — it's shaped through consistent learning, curiosity, and real-world action. Tools will change. Trends will shift. But the core mindset stays the same; stay adaptable, keep exploring, and commit to continuous growth.

Whether just starting or advancing along your path, let this guide be something you return to — a reference, a motivator, and a reset button when needed.

There's no perfect time to begin. Start where you are. Utilize what's available for you. Grow with the industry — and stay ready for what comes next.

Glossary of Common IT Terms

This glossary defines common IT terms used throughout the book. It's designed to help you quickly understand key concepts, tools, and acronyms — especially if you're new to the field.

Term	Definition
Artificial Intelligence (AI)	The ability of machines or software to mimic human intelligence, such as reasoning, learning, and problem-solving.
API	A set of rules that allows one software program to interact with another.
Agile	A flexible project management method that breaks work into short, iterative cycles called sprints.
BI (Business Intelligence)	Tools and techniques that are used to turn raw data into meaningful insights for business decisions.
Chatbot	An AI tool designed to simulate conversation and provide assistance or information (for example, ChatGPT, Gemini).
Cloud Computing	Using internet-based servers for storage, computing, and software delivery instead of local machines.
Copilot	An AI-powered coding assistant that suggests code snippets or functions inside your text editor.

CRM	(Customer Relationship Management) - Software used to manage a company's interactions with current and potential customers.
Cybersecurity	The practice of protecting systems, networks, and programs from digital attacks.
Database	An organized collection of data that can be accessed, managed, and updated.
DevOps	A set of practices that blends software development and IT operations to shorten the development lifecycle.
DNS	Domain Name System - translates website names into IP addresses.
Excel	A spreadsheet tool used widely for calculations, data analysis, and visualizations.
Firewall	A network security system that monitors and controls incoming and outgoing traffic.
Git	A version control system that is used to track changes in source code during software development.
Help Desk	The first line of IT support assisting users with technical problems.
IP Address	A unique string of numbers identifying a device on a network or the internet.
ITIL	A framework of best practices for delivering IT services.

Jira	A popular tool used in project and issue tracking, especially in Agile development.
KPI	Key Performance Indicator — a measurable value that shows how effectively a person or team is achieving goals.
Linux	An open-source operating system used widely in servers, cybersecurity, and development.
Machine Learning (ML)	A branch of AI that allows systems to learn from data and improve without being explicitly programmed.
Networking	Connecting computers and other devices to share resources and information.
Natural Language Processing (NLP)	A field of AI that enables machines to understand and generate human language (like ChatGPT).
PMP	Project Management Professional — a globally recognized certification for project managers.
Power BI	A Microsoft tool used to create dashboards and data visualizations.
Prompt	A question, instruction, or command given to an AI system to generate a specific response.
Prompt Engineering	The practice of designing effective prompts to get useful or accurate output from an AI tool.
Python	A beginner-friendly programming language used in automation, data analysis, and web development.

QA (Quality Assurance)	Processes and testing used to ensure the software works as intended.
SQL	Structured Query Language — used to access, manipulate, and manage data in relational databases.
SaaS	Software as a Service — software hosted in the cloud and accessed via a browser.
Tableau	A data visualization tool used to create interactive dashboards.
Ticketing System	Software used to track user issues.
Virtual Machine	A software-based emulation of a computer that runs an OS and apps like a physical machine.

Appendix

Free Learning Tools and Resources by Career Path

The following links include free tools, trial versions, and learning platforms to help you explore each IT path without needing to spend money upfront. Use these resources to get hands-on experience and start building your skills right away.

Support and IT Operations

- ServiceNow Developer Instance: https://developer.servicenow.com/
- CompTIA A+ Practice Labs: https://www.comptia.org/training/resources/practice-tests

Data and BI

- Tableau Public (Free): https://public.tableau.com/
- Power BI Desktop (Free): https://powerbi.microsoft.com/en-us/desktop/
- Kaggle (Data Projects and Datasets): https://www.kaggle.com/
- SQLBolt (Learn SQL): https://sqlbolt.com/

Cloud and DevOps

- AWS Free Tier: https://aws.amazon.com/free/
- Azure Free Account: https://azure.microsoft.com/en-us/free/
- GitHub Student Developer Pack: https://education.github.com/pack
- Codecademy – DevOps Path: https://www.codecademy.com/learn/learn-devops

Cybersecurity

- TryHackMe: https://tryhackme.com/
- Hack The Box (Beginner Labs): https://www.hackthebox.com/
- Cybrary (Cybersecurity Courses): https://www.cybrary.it/
- Google IT Support Security Path: https://grow.google/certificates/it-support/

Software and Web Development

- Visual Studio Code: https://code.visualstudio.com/
- GitHub: https://github.com/
- FreeCodeCamp (Full Web Dev Curriculum): https://www.freecodecamp.org/
- MDN Web Docs: https://developer.mozilla.org/

Programming Languages

- Python (Interpreter and packages): https://www.python.org
- Java (OpenJDK): https://openjdk.org
- JavaScript (Browser-based): https://developer.mozilla.org/en-US/docs/Web/JavaScript

Project Management

- Trello (Free): https://trello.com/
- Jira (Free for small teams): https://www.atlassian.com/software/jira
- Scrum Training Series: https://scrumtrainingseries.com/

AI Tools

- ChatGPT (Natural language AI): https://chat.openai.com
- Gemini (Google's AI chat assistant): https://gemini.google.com
- Perplexity AI: https://www.perplexity.ai
- GitHub Copilot: https://github.com/features/copilot
- Notion AI: https://www.notion.so/product/ai

Index

A

Active Directory, 66, 79- 108
Angular, 29, 58, 72, 100
APIs, 30, 40, 68,- 133
   HTTP methods, 72
   JSON, 72
   REST APIs, 72
Artificial Intelligence, 54, 135, 187, 188, 197
Automation tools, 68
   Cypress, 68, 101
   Jira, 25, 66-98, 152-205
   Postman, 68, 96
   Selenium, 26, 68, 96, 131
AWS, 19, 35-56, 74-140, 178, 204
   EC2, 81, 110
   IAM, 81, 85, 110, 117
   S3, 81, 110
AWS Certified Cloud Practitioner, 129
AWS Certified Data Analytics – Specialty, 134
AWS Certified DevOps Engineer – Professional, 137
AWS Certified Machine Learning – Specialty, 134
AWS Certified Solutions Architect – Associate, 137
AWS Redshift, 74, 104

Azure, 19, 35-140, 163, 204
   Blob, 81, 110
   RBAC, 81
   VMs, 79, 81, 110
Azure Administrator Associate, 137
Azure AI Engineer Associate, 135
Azure Enterprise Data Analyst Associate, 134
Azure Monitor, 81

B

Banking, 53
Bash, 66-83, 109, 113
BigQuery, 74, 104
Blogs, 106, 124
Bootcamps, 125

C

CAIC™, 135
Career Paths, 64, 91
CBAP, 131
CCNA, 136
CCSP, 139
CEH, 118, 138
Certifications, 10, 61, 112-163, 184
Certified Scrum Master (CSM), 131
Certified Selenium Tester Foundation, 131

ChatGPT, 6, 183- 205
CISA, 139
CISM, 139
CISSP, 138
CKA, 138
Cloud Computing, 18-65, 80, 92, 109, 136, 198
CloudWatch, 81
Codingame, 170
collaboration, 55, 60, 100, 151
Collaboration, 2
Community Colleges, 125
CompTIA A+, 130, 203
CompTIA Security+, 138
CSS, 29, 72-132
Cybersecurity, 19-65, 84-138, 199, 204

D

Data tools
  Figma, 70
  Power BI, 31, 59, 70-133, 148, 201, 203
Datadog, 83
Debugging, 192, 193
Dice, 170
Docker, 56, 81-84, 101, 115
Documentation, 2, 97, 119
Draw.io, 87, 120

E

ECBA, 131
E-commerce, 54
EdTech, 55

ELK stack, 83
Essential Skills, 6
  AI Literacy, 6, 187, 188
  Communication Skills, 7
  Databases, 8, 72, 101, 160, 161
    MySQL, 32, 72, 101, 161
    NoSQL (MongoDB), 72
    Oracle, 32, 72, 132-161
    PostgreSQL, 32, 72, 101
    SQL Server, 72
  Digital Literacy, 6
  Microsoft Office Applications, 6
  Problem-solving Mindset, 7
  Troubleshooting, 7, 66, 162

F

Finance, 53
Flutter, 30, 72, 101
freeCodeCamp, 72, 133

G

GCP, 36, 81-119
Gemini, 6, 189, 190-205
Git, 72, 83, 100, 113, 152, 200
GitHub, 37, 72-83, 100-106, 113-115, 132, 152-190, 204, 205
GitHub Copilot, 183-190, 205
GitLab, 37, 83, 113, 114

Glassdoor, 170
Google Cloud Certified - Machine Learning Engineer, 135
Google Data, 75, 104, 133
Google Data Analytics Professional Certificate, 133
Google IT Support Professional Certificate, 129
Grafana, 83, 115
GSEC, 139

H

Hackathons, 152
HackerRank, 152, 170
Healthcare, 53
HTML, 29, 72, 99-132

I

IBM Data Science Professional Certificate, 133
Indeed, 170
Industry Trends, 49
   Automation, 19-37, 41-68, 82-113, 137, 152
   Intelligent Systems, 58
   Remote Infrastructure, 56
   Reporting, 58-74, 104
   Visualization, 58
Information Technology, 1, 14, 16, 46, 48, 53

Infrastructure, 15-22, 34-65, 77-92, 107-115, 136
Infrastructure as Code, 81, 83, 110, 115
   ARM, 81
   CloudFormation, 36, 81, 83, 110, 115
   Terraform, 36, 81, 83, 110, 115, 137
Infrastructure monitoring, 78
   Nagios, 78, 108
   PRTG, 79
   Zabbix, 79, 108
Interviews, 158, 165
   In-Person Interviews, 169
   Phone Interviews, 168
   Video Interviews, 168
IoT systems, 55
ISTQB Foundation Level, 130
IT Employers, 49, 50
   Consulting Firms, 52
   Large Enterprises, 50
   Nonprofit Organizations, 52
   Public sector, 52
   Startups, 51, 60
   System Integrators, 52
   Tech Companies, 50
IT Job Categories, 24
   AI and Machine Learning, 18, 21, 32-65, 75-91, 105, 134, 145
      Computer Vision Engineer, 33, 76

Index

Data Scientist, 21, 32-
   43, 74, 76
Machine Learning
   Engineer, 32, 33, 76
NLP Engineer, 33, 43,
   76
Research Assistant, 21,
   33, 76
Automation and DevOps,
   19-37, 44, 65, 82, 92,
   113, 137
Build and Release
   Engineer, 37, 82
CI/CD Engineer, 37, 44,
   82
DevOps Engineer, 22,
   37, 44, 82
Monitoring Engineer,
   38
Observability Specialist,
   38
Cloud Computing, 18, 22,
   35-65, 80-136, 198
Cloud Architect, 36, 43,
   119
Cloud Engineer, 22, 36-
   57, 80, 82, 137
Cloud Security
   Engineer, 36, 80
Site Reliability
   Engineer, 36, 57, 80,
   82
Solutions Architect, 36,
   40-59, 80, 86, 140
Cybersecurity, 19, 23, 38,
   44-65, 84-92, 116-138,
   199, 204
Ethical Hacker, 39, 85,
   138
GRC Analyst, 39, 44, 85
Penetration Tester, 39,
   84
Risk Analyst, 39
Security Analyst, 23, 38,
   44, 57, 84
Security Architect, 39,
   44, 57, 85
Security Awareness
   Specialist, 39
Security Engineer, 38,
   57, 84
SOC Analyst, 23, 38, 84
Data Management and
   Analytics, 18, 21, 30-42,
   64-102, 133
Business Intelligence
   (BI) Analyst, 31, 73
Data Analyst, 21, 31, 42-
   73, 101, 133, 163
Data Engineer, 31, 42,
   73
Data Quality Analyst,
   32
Data Scientist, 21, 32,
   33-43, 74, 76
Data Steward, 32
Database
   Administrator, 31

Machine Learning
Engineer, 32, 33, 75
SQL Developer, 21, 31, 73
Infrastructure and System
Management, 18, 22, 34, 43, 65, 77, 92, 107, 136
Data Center Technician, 35, 78
Infrastructure
Engineer, 35, 78, 80
IT Operations and
Monitoring, 35
Network Administrator, 34, 78
System Administrator, 34, 78, 136
Non-coding Tech Roles, 7, 20, 27, 64, 69, 91, 97, 131
Business Analyst, 20-41, 59, 69, 70, 97, 131
Product Manager, 28, 41, 59, 69, 97
Program Manager, 28, 69
Scrum Master, 29, 41, 69, 131
Systems Analyst, 28, 172
Technical Product
Manager, 28, 69
Technical Project
Manager, 28
Technical Writer, 29, 69

Quality Assurance and
Testing, 17, 20-41, 64-94, 130
Manual QA Tester, 26
Performance Tester, 26
QA Analyst, 26, 67
QA Automation
Engineer, 26
QA Lead, 27
Test Automation
Engineer, 26, 67
Test Manager, 27, 41
Software and Web
Development, 17-29, 42, 57-99, 132, 204
Backend Developer, 30, 71
Frontend Developer, 29, 71
Full-stack Developer, 30, 71
Mobile Developer, 30
Software Engineer, 30, 42, 71, 101
UI/UX Designer, 30, 42
Support and Operations, 16, 20-25, 41, 64, 65, 91, 92, 129
Desktop Support
Technician, 25, 66
Help Desk Technician, 25, 66
IT Operations
Specialist, 25, 43, 78
IT Service Desk Analyst, 25

IT Support Specialist, 25, 65, 163
NOC Technician, 25
System Architecture, 19, 23, 39, 45, 65, 86, 92, 118, 140
    Enterprise Architect, 40, 45, 86
    Integration Architect, 45, 86
    Solutions Architect, 36, 40-59, 80, 86, 140
    Systems Architect, 40, 86
    Technical Architect, 40, 86
ITIL Foundation, 130

J

JavaScript, 29, 68, 72, 96-100, 132, 133, 205
Jupyter, 76, 106

K

Kaggle, 75, 77, 104, 106, 152, 203
Key IT Functions, 16
- AI and Machine Learning, 18
- Data Management and Analytics, 18
- Software and Web Development, 17
Automation and DevOps, 19
Cloud Computing, 18
Cybersecurity, 19
Infrastructure, 18
Non-coding Tech Roles, 17
Quality Assurance and Testing, 17
Support and Operations, 16
System Architecture, 19
System Management, 18
Kubernetes, 57, 81-84, 115, 138

L

Learning Options, 123
Learning Plan, 144, 146
LinkedIn, 94, 142, 151-178
Lucidchart, 87, 120

M

mentorship, 177, 181
Meta Back-End Developer Professional Certificate, 132
Meta Front-End Developer Professional Certificate, 132
Microsoft 365 Certified Fundamentals, 130
Microsoft Certified Azure Fundamentals, 129, 161
Microsoft Copilot, 189
Miro, 70, 98
MLOps, 76, 106

N

Networking, 47, 66-85, 93, 107-117, 162, 201
  DHCP, 66, 78, 93, 108
  DNS, 66, 78, 85, 93, 108, 117, 193, 199
  IP addressing, 66, 78, 107
Notion, 98, 152, 191, 205
Notion AI, 191, 205
NumPy, 74, 76, 104, 105

O

Operating systems, 66, 78, 83
  CentOS, 78
  Linux, 34, 66, 78-117, 136, 138, 201
  Red Hat, 78, 136
  Ubuntu, 78
  Windows Server, 78, 136
Oracle Certified Professional, 132
Oracle Database SQL Certified Associate, 134
OSCP, 139

P

Pandas, 74, 104, 105, 134
Perplexity AI, 190, 205
Playwright, 68, 96
PMI-CAPM, 131
portfolio, 71, 75, 82, 125, 142, 147, 159, 167, 173, 178, 182
PowerShell, 58-81, 94-113
Problem solving, 2
Prometheus, 83, 115
PyTorch, 18, 33, 76

Q

qTest, 96
Quality Assurance (QA), 26, 67, 94

R

React, 29-58, 72, 100-132
React Native, 30, 72, 101
Relevant, 159, 177
Replit Ghostwriter, 189
RHCSA, 136
Role of IT, 15
  Development and Data, 15
  Infrastructure and Operations, 15

S

scikit-learn, 18, 33, 76
SDET, 67
Skill Path
  AI and Machine Learning
    Computer Vision, 33, 76, 106
    Data Cleaning, 105
    Large Language Models, 106
    ML Libraries and Tools, 106
    MLOps, 76, 106
    Project Building, 106

174 | Index

Automation and DevOps
  CI/CD Concepts, 113
  Containerization, 115
  Orchestration, 115
  Version Control, 100, 113
Cloud Computing
  Cloud Monitoring, 110
  Containers, 83, 111
  Identity and Access Management, 110, 117
  Infrastructure as Code, 81, 83, 110, 115
  Major Cloud Platforms, 110
  Serverless, 111
Cybersecurity
  antivirus, 7, 108, 117
  firewall systems, 117
  Incident Response, 85, 117
  Nmap, 117
  Wireshark, 85, 117
Data Management and Analytics
  Data Fundamentals, 102
  Data Visualization Tools, 103
  Data Warehousing, 104
  Excel, 2-13, 21, 31, 59, 66-121, 142-159, 161-168, 189, 199
  Reporting Automation, 104
  Structured Query Language, 103, 202
Infrastructure and System Management
  Hardware, 107
  Networking Fundamentals, 93, 107
  Operating System Basics, 93, 107, 117
  Patch Management, 108
  Permission Management, 108
  Security Practices, 108
  Server Management, 108
  System Administration, 93, 108
Quality Assurance and Testing
  Bug Tracking Tools, 95
  Software Testing, 95, 130
  Test Case Design, 95
  Testing Types, 95
Support and Operations
  Help Desk Procedures, 94
  IT Service Management, 93
  Microsoft Office Tools, 93
  Networking Fundamentals, 93, 107

System Administration
  Basics, 93
  User and Device
    Management, 93
System Architecture
  Architecture Patterns,
    119
  GraphQL, 119, 193
  microservices, 87, 119
Specialization, 180, 181
SSCP, 139
Stackdriver, 81
Structured Training, 124
Summary, 160, 161
Supply Chain, 55
System Architecture, 19, 23,
  39, 45, 65, 86, 92, 118, 140

T

Tableau, 31, 59, 74, 98-148,
  161-168, 202, 203
Tableau Desktop Specialist,
  133
Tech Recruiters, 170
TensorFlow, 18, 33, 76
TestLink, 96
TOGAF 9 Certification, 140
TOGAF framework, 87

U

University Programs, 125
Upskill, 180

V

Virtualization, 78, 108
  Hyper-V, 78, 109
  VirtualBox, 78
  VMware, 78, 109
Visio, 87, 120
Vue, 29, 72, 100

W

Web frameworks, 72
  Django, 72
  Express, 72
  Flask, 72
  Spring Boot, 72
Windows Server Hybrid
  Administrator Associate,
  136

Y

YouTube, xvi, xx, 9, 124, 142

Z

Zephyr, 68, 96

www.ingramcontent.com/pod-product-compliance
Lightning Source LLC
Chambersburg PA
CBHW020412080526
44584CB00014B/1286